Embodied God in Indian Eco-Vision

Engaging with Śrī Rāmānuja's Theology

Interfaith Treasures Uncovered

Under this Series, the Publishers endeavor to focus on Comparative Studies pertaining to Christian Faith & Living in the central matrix and Hinduism, Buddhism, Sikhism, Islam, Judaism, etc., on the peripheral. The Studies shall cover topics like Literature & Poetry, Indigenous Philosophizing, Ethical response towards Agriculture, Health & Healing, Science & Technology, Ecofeminist Theology, Sociological approach towards Human Rights, Law & Politics, Arts, History of Ideas, Ancient Civilizations, Cultural Contiguity, Religious Cosmologies & Mysticism, Footsteps of famous Theologians, World Peace & Harmony, Global Capitalism, Network Marketing, Cybertheology, Population & Demographics, Epigraphic Studies, Contextualized Education, and many others. We welcome a Mss. on any topic/s mentioned, whether they are original works, scholarly monographs, collections of conference papers, revised dissertations, or translations of historical documents. Through the Series, we are striving to put forward published works that may help Institutions, Academic Bodies, Researchers, Scholars and the World at large in furthering their respective knowledge and understanding on the concerned subject. We welcome your comments on our efforts and further suggestions on how we can foster the upcoming books on parallel interfaces between and among Christianity and other religions.

Interfaith Treasures Uncovered - 19

Embodied God in Indian Eco-Vision

Engaging with Śrī Rāmānuja's Theology

Eric J. Lott

Foreword by
Israel Selvanayagam

CWI

Christian World Imprints

First Published in 2019 by

Christian World Imprints
Christian Publishing & Books from India
Shop No. 14, Ground Floor
C-3, Wazirpur Industrial Area
Delhi-110052
cwidelhi2017@gmail.com
info@christianworldimprints.com
www.ChristianWorldImprints.com

ISBN: 978-93-5148-369-4

Printed in India.

Contents

Foreword

Few will feel humbler than a student being asked by his own teacher to write a foreword to his masterly book. I first saw Dr. Eric J Lott in a conference on Hindu influence on Christianity in 1978 at the Tamilnadu Theological Seminary, Madurai. After completing my basic theological education and ministerial training, I had just started venturing into a new and challenging journey of interreligious dialogue and was badly in need of clarity, direction and encouragement. It was not a coincidence that I joined the United Theological College, Bangalore in 1981 for my Masters with specialisation in Hindu Religious Traditions. Eric Lott was the head of the department of Religions, Culture and Society. He was openly acknowledged as a great resource person especially for those students who came from villages with little competency in the English language.

Also, his special area of 'Vedāntic Approaches to God' could be quite intimidating for learners if not handled with encouragement and pastoral care, which he was able to. At the time we were three 'scholars in the making', and could notice that he gave great importance to Rāmānuja, particularly his scriptural hermeneutics and the central vision of God-Viṣṇu seen as having the whole world as his body. This vision made ideas such as *avatāra* and *bhakti* much more meaningful. Lott's publications and engagement with experts of the Śrī Vaiṣṇava tradition were evident of this shift, even though inadequately appreciated either by the college community or by the church. Memorably, he organised a study tour to Melkote (in Karnataka), an exclusively Śrī Vaiṣṇava village with a Brahmanic ethos. There we met his friend M.A.Thathachar, a most impressive teacher-priest with erudite knowledge of the Vaiṣṇava faith and tradition. The temple there too had special features with Rāmānuja as the central image.

Skipping a long journey, it so happened that I was able to follow him to England after he had left India in 1988 (while I was in the middle of my doctoral research), where I also worked as teacher and minister (in his Methodist church) from 1996. It was most encouraging and useful to consult him as teacher, colleague and friend. He was concerned about developing resources in the area of religions in theological seminaries in India and this was partly the reason that I went back in 2008 to teach at UTC and later at Gurukul Chennai for six years.

Around that time Brian Dunn's successful PhD dissertation (Oxford, 2013) on *The Body of God in Word, World and Sacrament: A comparative study of A.J. Appasamy and his reading of Rāmānuja* came out, signalling a revival of Rāmānuja study. In this there were very positive references to Lott's earlier studies, which was a causative factor in his deciding to bring out a collection of some of his most resourceful essays. The intention was to make a contribution not only in commending Rāmānuja's 'vision, tradition and interpretation' but also to the ongoing cry of environmental concerns all over the world. Illness prevented this from being realised in time for the celebration of Rāmānuja's birth-millenium in 2017. It should be noted that his wife Chris was, as ever, fully supportive of this writing project.

The millennium of Rāmānuja's birth in 2017 was marked with great celebrations and deliberations. But I want to note the two most remarkable events. First, the construction of a spectacular statue of Rāmānuja in Muchintal village, a few miles from Hyderabad International Airport. Crafted in China, the 'Statue of Equality' will be part of a temple complex: A towering 216-feet-high *panchaloha* which will be the second biggest in the world (next to the sitting statue of Buddha in Thailand), forming the centrepiece of a Rs.1,000 crore complex of 108 temples. Sixty specialist Chinese workers, engineers and welders will assemble the statue with digital sound and light show at the base of the statue (Ref. Serish Nanisetti, "A towering tribute to Bhakti saint Rāmānuja", *THE HINDU*, 10 December, 2016).

Secondly, M. Karunanidhi (1924-2018), a veteran leader of the Dravidian movement, playwright (of about 80 Tamil films), inspiring orator and writer, five-time chief minister of Tamil Nadu, was an avowed atheist. But he claimed that Rāmānuja was close to his heart and significant to his movement. In connection with his own 91st birthday his public address took the audience by surprise as he was referring to earlier Rāmānuja studies in Tamil, some of which were done in prison by those involved in the national movement for India's independence. Later, when the millennium approached, he penned a popular tele-series on the life of Rāmānuja. It is not clear what exactly prompted him to do all this. Some suggest a combination of the appeal of Tamil bhakti literature *Nālāyiradivyaprabhandham*, a connection with Śrī Rangam, the Dravidian movement's openness to philosophical thought, religious or secular, and Rāmānuja's efforts to transcend caste and the tradition of keeping sacred mantras in secret. It was not surprising that when Karunanidhi died the 'Centre of Ālvārs' (12 Vaiṣṇava saints) in Chennai organised a memorable event.

In the light of the above events, this book provides the theological basis for the millennial celebration and calls for a commitment for protecting the universe with reverence and love. The first chapter is a detailed introduction to Vedāntic traditions and their theologies. The second chapter introduces the core teaching of Rāmānuja, namely, God's relationship with the world and all life just as the soul relates to the body of a human being. The author notes that while God resides in the body and controls it, he is not in any way affected by the changes and actions of the body. A chapter points to the iconic vision of the heavenly forms of the glorious Lord, surrounded by myths and rituals, followed by the significance of divine grace and its manifestation in *avatāra*, creatively connected with the core vision of the universe as God's embodiment or his epiphanic body. The ecological implications of this vision and worldview are pointed out in changing eco-faith perspectives, particularly in India where there has been marked shift from exclusive liberation theologies to inclusive eco-theology. The climax, of course, is 'love-drowned' *bhakti* which celebrates creation as divine playfulness, inspires openness and transcendence in actual relationships in community.

This book results from a long and sustained engagement with Vedāntic traditions and their theologies, particularly the Vaiṣṇava theology of Rāmānuja. It is not only informative but stimulates further engagement with this theology. The beauty and embellishment of the metaphysical and *bhakti* language can be a great source for any theist. Rāmānuja has carefully crafted narratives from the Upaniṣads and the Bhagavad Gītā. For example, we read in the Gītā, in the context of the *viśvarūpa-darśana* Sanjaya declares: 'If the splendour of a thousand suns were to blaze forth all at once in the sky, that would be like the splendour of the Mahātman' and Arjuna exclaimed: 'You are the Imperishable, the Supreme Being to be realised. You are the great Treasure house of this universe; You are the imperishable Guardian of the Eternal Dharma' (11:12, 18). Such verses are taken as examples of perceiving God-Viṣṇu's supremacy - the other component of which is his accessibility, inseparability or intimacy. Numerous metaphors are used to describe this and the most poignant one is 'Friend', signifying the receiving of grace and drowning in love.

Eric Lott has engaged faithfully with Rāmānuja's 'Eco-Theology' without moving into a 'methodological agnosticism'; he has retained an acute awareness of his identity as a Christian minister, and as a Methodist for whom 'love divine, all loves excelling' is an existential compulsion. At the same time, he has never slipped into being negatively biased, never distorting his subject of inquiry. Here he has set a model for all those who have an extraordinary commitment to engage with the core vision and ethos of other religious traditions for mutual broadening and enrichment.

Finally, Lott's engagement encourages us also to engage further with the Vaiṣṇava (Śaiva and others), and this will mean asking further questions for clarification, a questioning which the author himself refers to at more than one point. Put very briefly, I would raise the following issues:

First, in Rāmānuja's vision of God as one inseparably holding within his being the whole universe and all life, and ruling that body, how can he not be responsible for the suffering in that body? The issue becomes especially problematic for those who see God as suffering in solidarity with the victims of oppression and injustice. As Lott notes, Śaiva Śiddhānta does not accept an avatāric body as the process of *karma-saṃsāra* is too limiting and makes for a defective state. And any doctrine of God being really incarnate calls for theological subtlety. Similarly, the idea of unconditional grace, of God accepting us without reserve, is one that for Christians as well as others has to be struggled with in its outworking.

Then, Rāmānuja's action of hosting a low-caste person at home at the cost of losing his wife was very radical in his time, and it is important to investigate his legacy in the Śrī Vaiṣṇava communities today. Sadly, caste continues to be rock solid in Indian society. Christians (so also other minorities) have failed to create a caste-free community. The actual impact of Rāmānuja's interpretation and his legacy on this issue calls for further study. Then, the role of sacrifice within the Vaiṣṇava community, in spite of challenges from the *bhakti* movements, raises questions. How Rāmānuja made efforts to reconcile ritual power and the power of a supreme Person is an important question to explore.

In following through these and similar questions no doubt we will all have opportunities to explore beliefs and practices in our own traditions which may lead to reformation. May Eric Lott's theological engagement continue to stimulate this kind of further engagement!

Evesham, UK **Israel Selvanayagam**
Pentecost, 2019

Preface

Impact from Afar: A Personal History

Two years ago the 1,000th anniversary year (2017) of the birth of that remarkable Indian theologian, Rāmānuja, was celebrated. The essays in this collection are offered in appreciation of his teaching. Perhaps, I can be forgiven brief reference to some of the personal background lying behind this concern. It was at theological college in London in 1958 that I first heard about this Vaiṣṇava community leader from South India. Both R.C. Zaehner at Oxford and Ninian Smart, then at London, had pointed to his significance for our understanding of God and the universe. In India, Bishop A.J. Appasamy long before had been urging Christian theologians as well as others to take note of Rāmānuja's thought about God and world – and I was privileged to meet the Bishop in 1960 and talk about these issues. Then, very recently the penetrating study at Oxford of Appasamy and Rāmānuja by Brian Dunn (see bibliography) makes their importance very clear.

For me, three emphases by Rāmānuja attracted:

(a) The vision that cosmic life is animated by and dependent on the Lord and inner Self of all, as a body is to its animating soul;

(b) The insistence that the binding heart of this cosmic life is mutual Love – God's compassion for all, and the heart's response of love for God;

(c) Then came Rāmānuja's bold insistence that all life, material and spiritual (even our mis-perceptions!) – *everything* is quite real, not a vain illusion, which seemed to me an equally crucial position to hold.

The appeal for me in this threefold vision in turn reflects both my organic farming background and the religious life in which I was nurtured. As a Methodist, that early experience was infused by the 18th century Wesleys' emphasis on divine love. Love was all-important. These founders of my spiritual tradition focussed on the 'heart', a centre of personal being that was to be under the sway of that divine love. In other words, theirs was a form of what Indian tradition has called 'love-devotion', or *premā-bhakti*.

Then, too, the Wesleys also insisted that this passionate love be grounded firmly in our relating to others in a very real world, materially and socially. For them, naturally, the embodying focus of this 'Love divine' was Jesus – whose very human birth, life-deeds and death ensured a faith-realism similar to that of Rāmānuja. The *reality* of our bodies, our society, our world is assured – wholeness of our human life is paramount. Then, to love God with 'all our mind' was also crucial to the Wesleys - John Wesley being a competent scholar in more than one field. The mind, too, is God-given and is to learn the ways of love!

By the 1970s and 1980s, I was teaching Indian Religious Traditions at colleges in South India. There, Śrī-Vaiṣṇava scholars were gracious enough to invite me regularly to present a paper in seminars held for their Pandits from all over India. (I especially thank Professor M.A. Thathachar, who came from Melkote, Karnataka, where Rāmānuja, having to flee from Śrī-Rangam, Tamilnadu, had sought shelter from the violent persecution of a king of a different religious tradition).

In one of these Vaiṣṇava seminars, following my presentation, a participant raised the question: 'But is Dr Lott not a Christian?' A reply came immediately from another of the Pandits: 'No doubt, though in his previous life he must have been a Śrī-Vaiṣṇava!' I took this to mean he approved of my interpretation of his Āchārya!

But, this takes us some way forward in the story of my love-affair with the teaching of Rāmānuja.

Re-reading the essays in this collection, and noting especially my frequent approval of Rāmānuja's detailed critique of the teaching of certain other *darśanas*, I can understand the Pandit's perplexity. It wasn't merely because of this young westerner's fluent quoting of numerous passages of their Ācārya's Sanskrit. It was also because my stance showed a very *pro-Rāmānuja bias*, and this is a theological bias I still maintain concerning key aspects of the Viśiṣṭādvaita vision of God.

Increasingly through the years, however, I have realised that, along with all our theologies, we also inherit *social and cultural* assumptions which we find very difficult to challenge. Our deeply embedded sense of identity is often very firmly embedded, and difficult to change. Yet, just such self-questioning is what faith in divine love calls for. As with a number of the passionate *bhakti*-poets of Indian religious history, however crucially important our social tradition may be, how is it possible to remain fully satisfied with our inherited social and cultural stance? We all need to move on to a deeper understanding of the *meaning* and the dynamic of divine love.

And, especially when there is – as with Rāmānuja – a vision of God embodied in the *realities of this world*, a world with monstrous socio-economic inequalities, should this not bring an even greater challenge for our traditional views of any established order of things? No doubt these two perspectives have led to some degree of tension within most religious histories – certainly within both Hindu and Christian traditions. From time to time, even religious leaders have been concerned to introduce reforms, and have questioned in a radical way the established order, the *dharma*, of their institutions.

When asked early in the 1960s to teach in a Telugu-medium theological college in South India, I was already primed with a pro-Rāmānuja bias. Along the way there were also Sanskrit studies; first at SOAS, London, then in India with Professor N.S. Anantarangachar, then at the Bharatiya Vidya Bhavan, Bangalore. Telugu religious language is so loaded with Sanskrit that the learning of this classical Indian language was not a great problem. In addition, I was able to have two one-year periods of intense research in Vedāntic writings (with Ninian Smart at Lancaster). Along with this – and related at a deep level of my being – was an increasing love of the natural world (birdlife especially), and engagement at depth with Indian people of hugely varied social and cultural backgrounds. All this led inescapably to a passion to probe more fully Rāmānuja's body-of-God vision of cosmic life.

Such probing has led to even greater admiration for this 1000-year old theological genius. At the same time, there was the need to pose the question I hint at above: was Rāmānuja's a sufficiently *dynamic* understanding of the ways of divine providence and divine grace? Is it possible that Rāmānuja's commitment to the given *dharma* of things would have been less unwavering if he had been more fully influenced by the *bhakti* poets that were such a prominent part of his Tamil Vaishnavism? For, the Ā<u>l</u>vārs' *bhakti* was a God-inspired passion that sometimes burst out in socially unpredictable ways. Had he expressed his faith-vision in their *poetic* form rather than in theological prose, would this perhaps have led to a less fixed view of the social order?

True, Rāmānuja himself at one point had a Guru who was a Sūdra (a fact his wife found unbearably difficult!). And those 'final words' of the Bhagavad Gītā (18.66) were of great importance to Rāmānuja: 'Give up all your *dharmas*, take me alone as your refuge….' As an Ācārya, his interpretation of this verse shows he had difficulty in taking the words at face value. Even so, it is a historical fact that Rāmānuja, when made leader of the great Vaiṣṇava centre of Śrī-Rangam, gave a considerable role to those from so-called 'lower' communities.

And yet, if a theology of the absolute *reality of things as they are* also led to an *absolutising of given structures* and traditions, is not the free working of divine grace thereby sorely strained? Our theological realism should never stand in the way of the dynamic ways of divine grace.

In spite of what may be seen as a slight diminishing of my passion for Rāmānuja's formal theological system, it still retains enormous appeal. I may even be far less critical (less critical than Rāmānuja was too) of Śaṅkara's transcendentalist Advaita than I was in the past, but there is still no doubt concerning which stance, ontologically, is the more convincing to me – as one for whom the passion of divine love remains a central tenet.

No doubt devotees of either Vedāntin will say that it matters little what the judgement of an 'outsider' may be! It is worth noting, however, that the great majority of 'outsiders' (i.e. not born into an Indian cultural tradition) who turn to Buddhist and Hindu spirituality in their search for truth and reality, seem far more convinced by an advaitic self-interiorising than by Rāmānuja's passionate focus on the personal being of God. I remain not so convinced.

The essays included in the collection that follows are all greatly modified forms of previously presented and, in most cases, published material. In cases where needed, permission to use in this revised form has been received. In addition to essays expounding Rāmānuja's thought, frequently comparing his position with other key Indian teachers in Vedānta (mainly Śaṅkara and Madhva), I include cross-cultural 'interfaith' attempts of mine that look considerably wider.

Being essays and lectures given at various times and in very different places, there is, inevitably, some overlap of key themes. This overlap has only partially been removed, as in each case common themes appear in distinct contexts, and within differing ways of understanding their significance.

In the Introduction both the 'Life and Writings of Rāmānuja' and 'Summary of Vedārtha Saṃgraha' are based on material in my *God and the Universe in the Vedāntic Theology of Rāmānuja,* Chennai: Rāmānuja Research Society, 1976.

(1) 'Vision and Doctrine in Vedanta' was a paper presented at the C.P. Ramaswami Foundation, Chennai in 1982; not previously published.

(2) 'Rāmānuja's Core-Teaching: The Body-Self Relationship' – first published in *Rāmānuja Vāṇī*, Chennai: Rāmānuja Research Society, 1982.
(3) 'Iconic Vision and World-View in Rāmānuja's Vedānta'– considerably revised version of a chapter included in my *Vision, Tradition, Interpretation: Theology, Religion and the Study of Religion,* Berlin: Mouton de Gruyter, 1988.
(4) 'Divine Grace in Indian Religious Traditions' – earlier version published in *Brahmavādin,* Vol.14, 1979.
(5) 'The Meaning of *Avatāra* in Indian Faith-Traditions: Rāmānuja's Realism' – earlier version published in *Dialogue & Alliance*, Vol. I, New York: IRF, 1987.
(6) 'Interpreting an Upaniṣad from a Viśiṣṭādvaita Perspective' – earlier version originally presented at an interfaith seminar at Westminster College, Oxford, 1994, then published in *Spiritual Traditions: Essential Visions*, a Festschrift for David Scott, edited by D.E. Singh, Bangalore: UTC, 1998.
(7) 'The Epiphanic Body: How Images & Concepts Relate' – earlier version first in *Mission with the Marginalised*, edited by S. Meshack, Thiruvalla: CSS, 2007.
(8) 'Changing Eco-Faith Perspectives in India' – earlier version published in a Festschrift for Gnana Robinson, *The Bible Speaks Today,* edited by D. Muthunayagam, Bangalore: UTC, 2000.
(9) 'All Loves Excelling: Dialogue on *Bhakti*' – earlier version in *A Great Commission: Christian Hope and Religious Diversity*, a Festschrift for K. Cracknell, edited by M. Forward, Stephen Plant and Susan White, Bern (Berlin): Peter Lang, 2000.

I thank those publishers who gave permission to reproduce materials from their publications. I also acknowledge with thanks the help of Israel Selvanayagam, both for urging me initially to publish these essays and for making suggestions for changes in the early stages. I am especially grateful to him for his kind

Foreword. For the preparation of the final draft I am also indebted to my son-in-law, Brent Ediss. Finally, let me record my thanks to the publisher, Christian World Imprints, New Delhi, for their fine presentation.

Eric J. Lott
Old Dalby, Leicester

Introduction

I. The Life and Writings of Rāmānuja

Vaiṣṇava tradition[1] states that Rāmānuja was born in 1017 CE at Śrī Perumbudūr, twenty-six miles from Madras, and died in 1137 CE at Śrī-Rangam, Tiruchirapalli. Inevitably, not everyone accepts these dates precisely as they stand, but there is little definite historical evidence to provide greater precision.[2]

The Vaiṣṇava Āḻvār saints[3] had stirred Tamilnadu from about the fourth to the eighth centuries with their fervent message of divine grace. Of the twelve remembered in the Vaiṣṇava tradition we may mention Bhaktisāra, Tirumangai, Nammāḻvār and the woman among them, Āṇḍāl. It was the task of the Ācāryas later to consolidate the Āḻvārs' influence and systematise their teachings, and thus strengthen the sacramental bond which the Śrī-Vaiṣṇava community experienced with them. The first Ācārya, Nāthamuni, a Brahmin adept in both Yoga and Nyāya, gathered the devotional songs of the Āḻvārs together in the *Nālāyira-divya-prabandham* ('Sacred collection of the 4000'). Eventually Nāthamuni became the administrative authority, as well as principal teacher, of the temple at Śrī-Rangam. Establishing the *Vedic* Orthodoxy of Śrī-Vaiṣṇavism seems to have been a major concern. His dates are given as 823 to 923 CE.

Nāthamuni's grandson, Yāmuna, was the second Ācārya of Śrī-Rangam. He went further in giving a Vedāntic form of expression to Vaiṣṇava doctrine, especially in his *Siddhi-traya,*[4] which is only partly extant. We also have his defence of Pañcarātra sectarian metaphysics and ritual, which he called Āgama-prāmāṇya.[5] His dedication to the *Bhagavad Gītā's* teaching is seen in his *Gītārtha-saṃgraha,*[6] and his devotional attitude in *Stotra-ratna.*[7] His life span is given as 916—1036 CE.

Rāmānuja, the third Ācārya, never met Yāmuna in person, but is said to have arrived at Śrī-Rangam just after Yāmuna's death, when he dedicated himself to carrying out the three unfulfilled wishes indicated by the three bent fingers of Yāmuna's corpse. The most important specific resolution was to write a full-length commentary on the *Vedānta-Śūtras.*

After his marriage Rāmānuja became a disciple of Yādava Prākāśa, who is referred to both as an Advaitin and a Bhedābhedavādin. In any case there was soon strong difference of opinion between Guru and Śiṣya, resulting eventually in Rāmānuja breaking with Yādava Prākāśa and joining a non-Brahmin disciple of Yāmuna's – Tirukacci Nambi at Kāñcipuram. Nambi instructed Rāmānuja to begin by carrying out the lowly task of bringing water from the well for the temple ritual. Despite the problem of Tirukacci Nambi being of a lower caste, Rāmānuja was fully intent on accepting him as Guru.

However, some tension resulted from this situation, especially because of Rāmānuja's wife's orthodox caste-consciousness, and eventually he was directed to Periya Nambi of Śrī-Rangam. There was an unexpectedly auspicious meeting of these two and Rāmānuja received the primary initiation into Śrī-Vaiṣṇava tradition from Periya Nambi. This included the branding of his shoulders, the marking of his forehead and the imparting of the secret *mantra.* After six months of instruction the wives of these two quarrelled over the question of their relative caste status, after which Rāmānuja sent his wife back to her home and became a Sannyāsī himself.[8]

Rāmānuja then began to lead a small monastic community in Kāñci, and even Yādava Prākāśa became one of his disciples. At this point Lord Ranganātha of Śrī-Rangam sent a message, through his priests, to Lord Varada of Kāñci, asking for Rāmānuja to be released for service to Śrī-Rangam. This was at first refused, but the dancing and singing of one of Yāmuna's disciples was so appreciated by Lord Varada that finally he acceded to the request.

Rāmānuja immediately took up the task of supervising the great temple at Śrī-Rangam. But his zeal in reorganising the administration was resented by the priests there and his taking over the temple leadership was far from smooth. There are somewhat conflicting versions[9] of what actually happened; in any case harmony was established eventually. Non-Brahmins were retained in various positions despite some pressure to change to an all-Brahmin administration. It is also probable that Rāmānuja was able to bring about greater co-operation between the more Vedic Brahmins and those more thoroughly steeped in the Śrī-Vaiṣṇava tradition.

But, Rāmānuja himself was still to be fully initiated into the more esoteric side of Śrī-Vaiṣṇava teachings. For example, Yāmuna's senior disciple, after keeping Rāmānuja waiting a long time, revealed the secret of *Guru-prapatti*, i.e., total dependence on the Guru as an *avatāra* of God. Then at Tirumalai, Rāmānuja's uncle taught him for a year the inner meaning of the Ramāyāna. The incident of the secret *mantra 'Om Namo Nārāyaṇāya'* taught by Tirukottiyur Nambi is of particular interest. Rāmānuja went eighteen times to him to learn this secret, each time being sent away disappointed. When finally the mystery was imparted, Rāmānuja went the very next day up on to a tower of *Śrī-Rangam* and proclaimed it to all the Śrī-Vaiṣṇavas gathered below. His defence for this action, done in defiance of his Guru's instruction, was that this means to salvation must be heard by all Śrī-Vaiṣṇavas, even if it meant his own damnation. On hearing this, Nambi confessed that he was 'unable to attain this fullness.'[10] Here we see again Rāmānuja's inclusive outlook, his life-concern for the divine revelation to be made available to as many as possible.

It was this concern that led Rāmānuja to tour various parts of South India and even further afield,[11] and to engage in philosophical disputes with scholars of different schools. There are various accounts given of his success in such debates, though in some cases it was some special manifestation of divine power which is said to have convinced his opponents, rather than his polemic ability. The debate with Śaivas at Tirumalai, for example, was decided by Venkaṭeśvara himself picking up the Vaiṣṇava emblems and wearing them in preference to the emblems of Śiva.

That Rāmānuja suffered various kinds of persecution seems well established. A number of years[12] had to be spent in exile from Śrī-Rangam in the Hoysala kingdom in Karnataka. One of the Cholas was so pro-Śiva that he commanded Rāmānuja to confess his faith in the supremacy of Śiva. Naturally he refused to do this. The action of his disciples (Periya Nambi being one) in taking his place, one of them disguised as Rāmānuja and even accepting the punishment of having his eyes gouged out, in order to ensure their Āchārya's escape, is a touching testimony to the strong loyalty Rāmānuja evoked.

While in the Hoysala kingdom, Rāmānuja was remarkably successful in winning over the Jainas to the Vaiṣṇava faith. Their king even assisted Rāmānuja in establishing a number of Vaiṣṇava temples in the region, with Melkote, not far north of Mysuru, being the best known of these. Many Jaina monks turned to Vaiṣṇavism, some whole-heartedly, some not. There are accounts of one thousand monks committing suicide rather than become Vaiṣṇavas, and of others being, 'ground to powder,' either by the over-zealous Viṣṇuvardana or by fellow-monks. These accounts should probably be taken metaphorically, though the fact is that killing in the name of religion (sadly as in many periods of human history) was far from uncommon at the time. Many accounts, however, stress the magnanimity of Rāmānuja towards defeated opponents. When the fanatic Chola king died, Rāmānuja was able to return to Śrī-Rangam where he eventually died in extreme old age, surrounded by many beloved disciples.

***Rāmānuja's works are*:**

(a) The *Vedārtha saṃgraha*[13] (lit. a 'Summary of the Meaning of the Vedas', i.e. 'Summary of Vedānta') a medium-length work and probably his first, deals systematically with most of the important issues in Vedānta. It is the only major work of

Rāmānuja's which is not based on any particular text, though parts of it are really commentaries on important Upaniṣadic texts. Hence it probably reflects Rāmānuja's own order of priorities, and I include below a precis of this 'Summary'.

(b) *Śrī-Bhāṣya*[14] is a full-length commentary on the *Brahma (or Vedānta)-Śūtras,* i.e., over 500 very short, and often enigmatic, statements, dating perhaps from around 200BCE, intended as encapsulations of the Vedāntic tradition. A notable feature is the great length of Rāmānuja's comment on the first *Sūtra* ('Then, therefore, the desire to know Brahman'). He there includes the *Mahā-Siddhānta*[15] ('Great doctrine') which has a detailed response to Advaita.

(c) *Vedānta-dīpa* and *Vedānta-sāra*[16] are two very brief commentaries on the same Śūtras. Their authenticity is questioned by some scholars.[17]

(d) Of all the classical commentaries, Rāmānuja's *Gīta-Bhāṣya*[18] is probably Vedanta's most authentic interpretation of the *Gītā's* original meaning.[19] There is a more clear *bhakti*-orientation than found in his *Śrī-Bhāṣya,* as is clearly reflected in the *Gīta-Bhāṣya's* opening *Mangala-śloka.* While many scholars stress Rāmānuja's indebtedness to Yāmuna's summary of the Gītā's teaching, that summary is so brief that Rāmānuja can hardly have been indebted to it for more than a general interpretative viewpoint. However, the oral initiation into the Vaiṣṇava interpretation, given by Yāmuna's disciples, may well have been more detailed and decisive.

(e) The *Gadya-traya* and *Nitya-grantha*[20] are shorter, more esoteric devotional works. The *Śaraṇāgati-gadya* ('Going for Refuge') in particular, being a dialogue between Rāmānuja and the divine couple Śrī and Lord Nārāyaṇa, plays an important role in the devotional life of Śrī-Vaiṣṇavas. It expresses the devotee's (Rāmānuja's) ardent desire for forgiveness, for enlightenment and the experience of total surrender to the Lord, who is initially approached through Śrī-Lakṣmi. Then the Lord graciously grants this request. *Śrī-ranga-gadya* is a prayer for acceptance as an eternal servant of the Lord. *Vaikuṇṭha-gadya* is a detailed description of Viṣṇu's eternal dwelling-place, and is to be meditated on after surrendering oneself in the act of *prapatti* ('Falling', i.e. at the feet of the Lord). The *Nitya-grantha* is a manual for daily non-temple worship by Śrī-Vaiṣṇavas, to be offered before the household or monastery image, or with a mental image held before one. There is no need here to enter the debate on the authenticity or otherwise of these more devotional writings.

II. A Summary of Vedārtha-Saṃgraha

A separate account of this brief (in Sanskrit 40 pages), yet relatively inclusive, exposition of the essentials of Vedānta (the 'end, or meaning, of the Vedas') is merited. Rāmānuja begins by pointing to the Upaniṣads as the key sources of Vedānta, though these texts, he claims, need to be properly interpreted, i.e., not as some forms of Advaita do. The texts are looked at both in the light of scripture and reason.

Then (in Raghavan's translation paragraphs 81ff) the key text '*Tat-tvam-asi*' (That thou art) is interpreted in line with the established grammatical principle of 'co-ordinate predication' – meaning there is 'inseparability' but not ultimate identity. The first of a string of texts (mainly Upaniṣads and Bhagavad Gītā, confirmed with a few Vaiṣṇava sources) quoted in support of his position is: 'He who dwells in the earth… whose body the earth is, and who rules the earth from within, he is thy *ātman*, the inner controller…' (Bṛhadāraṇyaka Upaniṣad V.7.3 etc).

Rāmānuja then argues that Brahman is not only efficient cause, but also the substantial or material cause of all that is. Indeed, every entity in its inmost being, and therefore every term naming those entities, points to the ultimate Cause and Goal of all, Brahman. (At this point, as on occasion elsewhere, reference is made to texts seeming rather esoteric to the modern mind, but obviously in the time of Rāmānuja used by those engaging in Vedāntic debate).

Then, in paragraphs 99-108 comes an important section beginning 'The heart of the whole *śāstra* is this...', with a very traditional 'Indian' account of our human condition: 'individual selves' in their essence are comprised of 'pure knowledge'; but this essential being is obscured by its opposite, *avidyā*, ignorance (often translated as 'nescience'), corresponding to the varying degrees to which each is in the grip of *karma-saṃsāra*, i.e., those bodily conditions each is born into in the cycle of birth and rebirth, and resulting in each person identifying with the particular bodily condition into which it is born. It is only through 'surrender to the supreme Lord' that each self can come to realise its true nature – each being essentially alike. 'The essential nature of the individual self is to be wholly subservient and instrumental to God and therefore with God as its inner self'. Rāmānuja hastens to add that the 'nature of that supreme Being is unique, being of absolute perfection, the absolute opposite of all that is evil...an ocean of countless, infinitely excellent attributes...'

Soon comes another key theme (in 103): Each self is 'wholly subservient to and controlled by the Lord, each one's sole support'. For, 'the individual self is the body of the Lord'. Here comes a quote from the Gītā: 'By me, in imperceptible form, this whole universe is permeated. All beings have their being in me; I do not have my being in them' (Gītā IX: 4-5). The Supreme Person, by his miraculous power, is both one and many.

After responding to various objections, in para 126 there is an important statement of Rāmānuja's theological position. (And we note that the Sanskrit in this section is made up of very long and complex terms, suggesting they are well-rehearsed theological statements). The essential point is the need for surrender to God in loving devotion, a deeply devotional *bhakti* that 'takes on the character of vivid and immediate vision. Through such *bhakti* is the Supreme attained'.

The numerous references in various scriptures to variously named deities, and even the meaning of the three-syllabled sacred syllable, AUM, are dealt with in several sections after this, in every case concluding that it is the one Brahman, the supreme Person, who is the one cause of creation and the one liberating goal of universal being. Paragraph 147 has an especially complete description of the greatness of Brahman. After this again a variety of objections are dealt with.

From Paragraph 167 onwards, Rāmānuja first argues against the theory of Prabhākar who taught the superiority of imperative *doing* – doing the sacred cultic action in particular, as enjoined in the *karma*-strand of the Vedas – i.e. the imperative to *do,* rather than indicative *knowing*. Then, there is a long discussion of the nature of words and the Word, and the need to find our ultimate destiny in 'the supreme Brahman, as infinite knowledge, infinite bliss, infinite purity...one by whose will all other entities... are sustained in their being...' (Paragraph 198 again contains massively complex Sanskrit compounds, suggesting another well-rehearsed faith-statement. We might also note paras 214-15 with an impressive exposition of *satya*, 'true/truth', especially in the description '*satya-sankalpa*', interpreted as bringing out the supreme Person's omnipotent will, that is able to control Nature, with her threefold properties, as the 'instruments of his cosmic play' or *līlā*) .

Again, after a number of points referring to esoteric issues, there is a mounting focus on the personal qualities of God, in increasingly Vaiṣṇava terms, and on the absolute need for a dependent attitude of sheer *bhakti* and the love-relationship this entails. While some deride the way of serving and dependence as 'a dog's life', Rāmānuja closes this Summary with the statement: 'In reality, only knowledge that is of the nature of supreme *bhakti* (i.e. loving devotion) is the means for attaining the Lord'.

Endnotes

1. The rich traditions relating to Rāmānuja's life have been conveniently gathered together by A. Govindacharya in *The Life of Rāmānujāchārya*, Madras: S. Murthy, 1906. and by C. R. Śrīnivasa Aiyengar in *The Life and Teachings of Śrī Rāmānujāchārya,* Madras: R.Venkateshvar, 1908.
2. J. Carman, *op. cit.*, pp. 27. 44-46, suggests 1077-1157 AD for Rāmānuja's life, but he admits he may have lived considerably more than 80 years. 'Unfortunately, however, it is very difficult to put all the dates given in the traditional biographies (some of them conflicting), inscriptional evidence

from Mysore, and our knowledge of the Cola kings of the period, together into one coherent pattern' (p. 44).

3. K. C. Varadachari's *Āḻvārs of South India,* Bombay: Bharatiya Vidya Bhavan, 1966, is a useful introduction to their teachings, though tending to 'philosophise'. J. S. M. Hooper's *Hymns of the Āḻvārs* is a translation of selected songs, with comments. A more complete publication is S. Bharati, *The Sacred Book of the Four Thousand. or Naalayira Divya Prabandham (An English translation with Tamil original),* Chennai: Sri Sadagopan Tirunarayanaswami Divya Prabandha Pathasala, 2000.
4. Edited and translated (with an introduction) by R. Ramanujachari and K. Srinivasacharya, Madras: Ubhaya Vedanta Grandhamala, 1972.
5. Ed. and trans. by J. A. B. Van Buitenen, Madras: Rāmānuja Research Society, 1971.
6. Included with translation in M.R. Sampat Kumaran's *The Gīta-Bhāṣya of Rāmānuja*, Madras: Rangacharya Memorial Trust, 1969.
7. Translated by Swami Adidevananda, Madras: 1967.
8. The Śrī-Vaiṣṇava Ācārya did not necessarily become a Sannyāsī, this being in sharp contrast to Śaiva tradition and Śaṅkara's system. Obviously the Vedāntic realism of Viśiṣṭādvaita is reflected in a more positive attitude to daily life and social relationships.
9. One version claims that Kūraṭṭālvān tricked the previous high priest into handing over the keys.
10. It is also said that Nambi embraced Rāmānuja and called him '*Emperumānār,*' 'Our Lord.'
11. He is said to have visited Kashmir and there to have read Bodhāyana's *Sūtra-Bhāṣya.* It had to be returned immediately, so Rāmānuja was dependent on Kūraṭṭālvān's incredible memory for later knowledge of it.
12. Twelve years according to the tradition.
13. Edited and translated by J.A.B. Van Buitenen (Poona, 1956); by S. S. Raghavachary (Mysore, 1956); and by M. R. Rajagopala Aiyangar (Madras, 1956). All Rāmānuja's works are available in the original, edited and collected in one volume, *Śrī Bhagavad Rāmānuja Grantha-māla* by P. B. Annangaracharya (Kanchipuram 1956).
14. Translated by G. Thibaut in *Sacred Books of the East.* Vol. XLVIII (Oxford 1904); by M. Rangacharya and M. B. V. Aiyangar (Madras 1961 to 1965).
15. Western scholars such as R. Otto and O. Lacombe regarded this one section as a treatise complete in itself.
16. The former has been translated by K. Bhāṣyam (Madras, 1959), and into German by A. Hohenberger (Bonn, 1960); the latter by M. B. Narasimha Ayyangar (Adyar 1953).
17. VS(VB), p. 32. He wonders why Rāmānuja should want to write such summaries of what was available fully in *Śrī-Bhāṣya,* rather than write commentaries on the Upaniṣads.

18. Translated by M. R. Sampath Kumaran (Madras, 1969).
19. Thus the conclusion of R. C. Zaehner in his important commentary *The Bhagavad-Gītā* (Oxford, 1969).
20. Only *Śaraṇāgati-gadya* is available in English. E.g., in *Viśiṣṭādvaita-philosophy and Religion* (Ed. V. S. Raghavan), translated by S. V. Śrīnivasan.

1

Vision and Doctrine in Vedānta

When India's great philosophers of the past referred to their systems as '*darśanas*', they imply, very rightly, that every conceptual system is built up around some prior *vision* of reality. There is first an inner intuited perception of how things are, and from this inner vision emerges the explicit system with its elaboration of concepts and arguments, its scriptural exegesis and doctrinal interpretation. *Darśana* is prior to *vāda* (argument); that which is taken as an established conviction (*siddha*) is prior to *siddhānta* (doctrinal system).

Another way of putting this is to say that in each developed religious tradition there is not only a doctrinal belief-system; we must also share in the creative visionary matrix of the tradition, its myths and rituals, the esoteric life by which the inwardness of the tradition is engaged with and transmitted. Naturally, this sets limits to the authenticity of an interpretation by an 'outsider', however well-based. That outside view, however, may also have something very significant to say, especially as the Śrī-Vaiṣṇava community seeks to interpret Rāmānuja in the world of today. It was for this reason, presumably, that during one of this tradition's all-India seminars, I was invited by a group of 'elders' to share possible insights into the communicating of religious tradition to estranged younger people in the community.

In any case, even though inner vision precedes belief-system, we cannot ignore the conceptualisations which have emerged in the course of interpreting our traditions. Doctrinal systems are far from telling the whole story – imagery, sacred places, sacred songs, myths and symbols are equally important. Yet, doctrine too is of great importance in understanding religious traditions. If Rāmānuja's vision of reality is communicable at all, he communicates it through his writings, through his conceptual articulation of the vision in *Śrī-Bhāṣya*, in *Gītā-Bhāṣya*, in *Vedārtha-Saṃgraha*, in *Gadya-Traya*, etc. All are replete with doctrinal undergirding.

And the same applies to other Vedantic systems, such as those of Śañkara, Nimbarka, Madhva, and Vallabha. Behind each system, determining its shape and conceptual structure, lies a creative vision. But each such conceptual structure must be taken seriously. We cannot assume, for example, that underlying the difference of the expressed doctrines there is somehow but one vision of reality, as many recent 'Hindu' religious teachers have assumed. This in effect, is claiming to know more about their vision than those Vedantic visionaries did themselves; it is to take a trans-visionary stance, which in effect is a new kind of vision. Such a stance has also tended to undermine rigorous research into the conceptual structure of the Vedantic systems, and modern Indian religious and theological scholarship has thereby been the poorer.

When Rāmānuja begins his great Vedantic *Bhāṣya* with such strongly worded criticism of certain other Vedāntic view-points, it was not because he was carried away by sectarian jealousy or some childish tantrum. It was a matter of ultimate importance to establish that his vision of reality was radically distinct from that of other systems, even other Vedāntic systems.

Common Vedāntic Issues

Most of the questions to which Rāmānuja responded were, of course, common Vedāntic questions; he worked within the

Vedāntic discipline. Indeed there are a number of answers too that are common Vedāntic answers to the mystery of existence. For example, there is:

(a) Acceptance of Vedānta's *prasthāna-traya* (the three foundations), taking the Upaniṣads, the Bhagavad Gītā and the Brahma-Sūtra as the canonical basis for constructing a Vedāntic system.
(b) There was the *pramāṇa-traya* (the three authoritative sources) with *pratyakṣa* or perception, *anumāna* or inference, and *śabda* or testimony as the means by which we acquire valid knowledge.
(c) There was acceptance that Vedānta begins with *Brahma-jijñāsa,* or the 'desire to know Brahman', the 'enquiry into Brahman'.
(d) This naturally takes for granted that *Brahma-jñāna* ('knowledge of Brahman') is of primary importance to Vedānta, and that this in some way contrasts with what is required by the 'action-section' of the Vedas.
(e) The *karma*-concept also involves the acceptance of the binding process of *karma-samsāra* (the cycle of births and rebirths resulting from action) and the need for *mukti* (release) from the bondage of the process. *Mukti,* however, is not the only *puruṣārtha* (goal of human life) acceptable to Vedānta – *dharma* too plays an important undergirding role.
(f) Then, Vedānta also accepts that in the process of seeking the highest 'goal of life', Brahman, the 'Great Self'. is to be understood as that ultimate life-goal.
(g) Various *yogas* and *sādhanas* (systems of discipline) are also taken by all Vedāntins as necessary for the task of reaching this goal, though in the final analysis only Brahman can enable the soul to reach himself; he is both goal and means.
(h) Then, too, Vedānta generally accepts that Brahman is the one 'cause of the world's origin, preservation and

destruction', i.e., the one ultimate Cause of the universe and its functioning.

(i) *Māyā* (originally 'supernatural power', later 'illusory') and *līlā* (playfulness) are also terms that all Vedantins use, even though often with very diverse meanings, especially *Māyā*.

(j) Then there is the fundamental distinction between *Prakṛti* (Nature) and *Ātmā* or *Puruṣa* ('self', 'person') a distinction that had been brought out forcefully by Sāṃkhya well before Rāmānuja. In Vedānta, however, the individual self is taken, in various ways, as being in some sense revelatory for understanding the being of Brahman, the *Parama-ātmā*, the 'Highest Self'.

Even as we list such common Vedāntic features, it is clear that their followers, i.e., the various Vedantins, interpret these themes rather differently. I would like, therefore, to draw out six aspects of Rāmānuja's thought that, I believe, make the most significant contribution to the Vedantic debate.

What is Brahman?

1. The first question of ultimate concern in the Vedāntic discipline seems simple enough: '*What is Brahman?*' That Brahman *is* cannot be doubted by a Vedāntin. His being is *siddha*, already established as an eternal entity. Nor can it be doubted that Brahman is the ultimate Reality, the irreducible Ground of all being, the *Sat* from whom all *sattva*-being derives (*satya,* or 'truth', too), the highest *Cit* (Consciousness) by which all living souls are conscious beings, the *Parama-ānanda*, the 'highest bliss' from which comes all lesser joys. Vedāntins sometimes bring forward very cogent arguments pointing to the existence of Brahman, usually as being the necessary source of existence, consciousness and bliss. Unexpectedly perhaps, it is in Śañkara's writings that we are most likely to come across such argumentation. It was Śañkara who gave greatest emphasis both to Brahman's self-authenticating ultimacy and to *anubhava* (inner experience) as the only ultimate means for the knowledge of Brahman.

That this 'Great Being' *is*, then, need not be argued, said Rāmānuja. But *what* Brahman is – that is a very different matter. Vedānta (in the Sūtras at least) begins with the statement, *athāto Brahma-jijñāsa*: 'Now, then, the enquiry into Brahman'. In responding to this question, Rāmānuja, as did Śañkara, began with the significance of the name 'Brahman'.

> The term "Brahman" denotes the highest Person, who is essentially free from all imperfections and is endowed with innumerable glorious qualities of incomparable excellence. For the term `Brahman' is applied to those things which possess the quality of greatness, i.e. *bṛhattva*; but it primarily denotes that which has greatness of essential nature, as well as of qualities, in unlimited fullness; and such only is the Lord of all (*Śrī-Bhāṣya* 1.1.1).

Brahman is the *Distinctively Great One*

Brahman, then, is the outstandingly, extra-ordinarily great One, the One than whom there can be no greater, no more wonderful Being. In other words, Rāmānuja begins with a view of Brahman as essentially distinguished by great qualities: One whose uncountable *kalyāṇa-guṇas* (auspicious, beautiful qualities) distinguish him as *Parama-ātmā* (highest Self), as *Puruṣa-uttama* (supreme Person). His glorious character makes him one to be adored, to be worshipped and to be *loved*. For, there is a deep mystery here: though transcendentally great, Brahman makes himself accessible to the devotion of those who come to love him. Or, as later Vaiṣṇavas put it, in a wonderful way Brahman exhibits both *paratva* and *saulabhya* dimensions (otherness and closeness) and neither dimension is to be lost in affirming the other.

What is especially significant in Rāmānuja's vision of Brahman's distinguished character is his insistence that this *sa-viśiṣṭatva*, this *sa-guṇatva* ('one with distinctive qualities') can never be superseded. We cannot graduate to some experience of One who is above all wonder-evoking personal attributes. Such an adorable nature, with all its specific glorious qualities, is how Brahman is, eternally and ultimately.

Here, of course, Rāmānuja is in direct confrontation with those whose 'Brahman' was of a radically different transcendental nature. And such confrontation was necessary for the integrity of his vision, a vision which is surely an essential dimension in so much Indian religious consciousness. For does not the oft-repeated argument of some non-dualists run as follows: 'Yes, at a certain stage in our religious pilgrimage, being limited human beings, we have to think of God as personal, as *sa-guṇa* (one with distinguishable qualities) but in order to attain the independence of true liberation, eventually we must free ourselves from all such limiting concepts, we must reach the freedom of experiencing Brahman as pure consciousness, as pure being, as *nir-guṇa* to whom no distinct qualities can be attributed?'

Of course, Rāmānuja was well aware that the mystery of God is such that our descriptive attributes can never exhaust his true nature, can never do him full justice. There is always more to be said. Hence, according to Rāmānuja, the Upanishadic negation of our descriptions of God, the '*neti, neti*' text, means: 'It is not only thus, but much more too'. However, this more-than-ness of God, for Rāmānuja, does not deny the truth of those wonderful qualities that the saints of the past have attributed to God according to their vision of his greatness.

How Do We Know Brahman?

2. There is another equally important Vedantic question: '*How do we know this Brahman*?' Or, 'of what kind is our knowledge of Brahman?' In one sense all Vedāntins begin, as we have already noted, with their pre-conceptual vision of God, an inner perception of ultimate reality that is taken as a presupposition upon which to ground their Vedāntic articulation. This ultimately self-authenticating *anubhava* (inner experience) is certainly of great significance in any tradition claiming knowledge of God. It is usually far more determinative of the way we construct our God-systems than are the formal *pramāṇas* (ways of knowing) we ostensibly agree to. Thus, even though Vedāntins claim that the being and nature of Brahman are known to us only through *śruti*

('scripture which is *heard*', i.e., the Vedas), none would take this in a crudely literal sense.

It is interesting that both Śaṅkara and Madhva – though disagreeing on so much - appear to give far more importance to direct vision or *immediate* perception (*aparokṣa-jñāna, sākṣātkāra*) in the process of knowing Brahman, than did Rāmānuja. Śaṅkara even goes to the extent of saying that our experience of self-consciousness in itself is enough to establish Brahman's existence. In other words, he virtually equates consciousness and ultimate being. And for him, true knowledge of Brahman is essentially that transcendent intuition of pure undifferentiated consciousness in which there is no vestige of the *relational* dimension of our human nature; the identity of such transcendent consciousness is the ultimate being we are to seek, according to Śaṅkara.

To Rāmānuja, saying that Brahman is pure consciousness, with no describably distinguishing features, makes no sense epistemologically. All the formally accepted means by which we know anything validly just do not lend themselves to knowing in such a way and knowing such an undifferentiable being. *Pramāṇa* and *prameya,* means and the End, must have some kind of commensurability. In modern communications jargon, the medium must conform to the message.

Even if we do not give final importance to the role of the *pramāṇas* in the process by which we know God, to claim that *Brahma-jñāna*, knowledge of the ultimate One, consists of pure consciousness, implied Rāmānuja, is to undermine all those religious values and the religious vision which is so prominent in the same Brahman-knowing process. For, essential to that process, as witnessed to by the Upaniṣads and in the experience of subsequent religious traditions, is *Brahma-upāsana*, that meditative worship of God's excellence out of which fuller knowledge of his nature arises. And such *upāsana*, argued Ramauja, culminates in the *bhakti-bhāva* of loving dependence and devout trust. For, an essential element in true knowledge of God is the awareness that we are utterly dependent upon him. He is *sva-tantra* (self-determined) we are *para-tantra* (other-determined) as Madhva was to stress even more strongly later.

An Inseparable Relationship

Then, Rāmānuja saw another equally important dimension in this knowledge of Brahman. Not only are we to see our dependence as essential and integral to true 'knowledge' of God; we are also to see that we are *inseparably related* to God. There is an *apṛthak-sambandha*, a relationship of 'inseparability'. To realise that we cannot exist for a moment separate from him is to be a true *jñānī*. Knowledge of God is to lead to *love* of God; indeed, ultimately, according to Rāmānuja, *jñāna* must be interpreted in terms of *bhakti*, i.e., truly to know God requires love for God. True *bhakti*, therefore, is not a matter of devoting oneself to God for what can then be received from him. True *bhakti*, the highest *parama-bhakti* is *sādhya-bhakti*, or, devotion to God entirely for his own sake; it is loving him because no other attitude is appropriate once we have seen his wonderful qualities. God's very nature is *bhakti*-evoking, especially *love*-evoking.

Based on Grace

And yet, such is the glory and greatness of that divine nature, and such the disparity between his love for us and our love for him, that the *bhakti*-life is ultimately dependent upon his mercy, his sovereign grace. Only an attitude of sheer surrender to that grace, or *śaraṇāgati-bhāva*, can provide a proper basis for our *bhakti*-relationship with God. It is of great significance that in his *Vedārtha-Saṃgraha* Rāmānuja, in a crucial paragraph describing knowledge as *bhakti*, twice states that taking *śaraṇāgati* ('going for refuge') at the feet of the Lord who then by his grace dispels all the darkness concealing the innermost self, is essential to the *bhakti* process. Only his grace is ultimately sufficient for souls to share in his divine qualities. The true *jñānī*, then, will begin as a *prapanna* ('one who falls at his feet'). Rāmānuja took with all seriousness the Gītā's *Carama-śloka*; which is said by Krishna to be his highest and most secret word:

Sarva-dharmān parityajya, mām ekam śaraṇam vraja;
aham tvam sarva-papebhyo mokṣayiṣyāmi, na sucaḥ.
(Give up all your dharmas, Take me alone as your refuge,
I will set you free from all your sin, Have no worry).

Before I leave this question of the nature of *Brahma-knowledge*, I should add a further word about knowledge as *aparokṣa*, or immediate. Rāmānuja too, like both Śaṅkara and Madhva, claimed that the loving meditation of the devotee who lives only for God consists of an inner perception of God that is quite *direct and uninterrupted*, i.e., it is *pratyakṣata* and *sākṣātkāra* in character. Yet Rāmānuja seems to be speaking of a special kind of immediate knowledge; for he cannot allow that the living, dynamic *relationship* between God and soul is ever superseded. His claim is that even within this essentially mediated relationship, there is *immediacy*. The true *bhakta*'s knowledge, then, is that of *mediated immediacy* (A description once used by Scottish Theologian, John Baillie, to define our 'Knowledge of God').

God as both Means and End, Way and Goal

3. This raises again the Vedāntic question of *sādhya* and *sādhana*: how does the ultimate Goal (God) relate to the means by which to attain this Goal. Clearly it is the Bhagavad-Gītā that raises this question most explicitly. For, in the Gītā we find the three ways (*mārgas* or *yogas* – i.e. *karma, jñāna, bhakti*) all given a significant role. This is not the place to attempt a comprehensive exposition of the meaning of the Gita, the 'Divine Song'. We should at least note that human action, like divine action, is given a highly significant role by the Gītā's author (Even though 'all *dharmas*' are eventually to be 'given up', according to a literal reading of the *Carama-śloka,* BhG.18.66). This does not mean, according to Rāmānuja, that all social duty, good human action, is as such to be given up; certainly the desire for personal benefit from our actions is to be renounced. Action is to continue, not least because (as the Gita says) *loka-saṃgraha*, or the integrating well-being of the world, is always a desirable good, and for this reason the Lord himself acts, and he is the One we are to emulate.

But Vedānta had long agreed that human action as such can never bring about the ultimate liberation the soul seeks. Indeed, each act of ours serves but to tighten the knot of *karma-bandha*, though our good action makes the bondage more bearable, even pleasurable. Only knowledge of that Being who transcends this karmic process, who himself operates it, can result in our ultimate liberation from such a process. The final 'goal for human good', then, is through *Brahma-jñāna*. And so all Vedantins agreed, though understanding this 'knowledge' differently.

Bhakti integrates the Three Ways

Then came two further questions: How does this *Brahma-knowledge* relate to the actions necessary to good human living, and how does it relate to the needed attitude of devotion? This latter question we have looked at already: for Rāmānuja, ultimately *Brahma-jñāna* equals God-*bhakti* (true 'knowledge of the Great One' means 'loving devotion'). But what of human action? Here Rāmānuja brought out the simple fact that any true devotee of God will want to please God by good works, and that such good deeds for an authentic ethical life are to spring from the conviction that when we do our *dharma* we are in tune with the ultimate cosmic Reality.

Thus, for Rāmānuja, *bhakti* becomes the key to the integration of the three ways (*mārgas or yogas)*. It is the one who loves God who truly knows God, and one who loves God will do all good works pleasing to God. Although disagreeing with Bhāskara's synthesis of action and knowledge (*karma-jñāna-samuccaya*), by taking *bhakti* as the determining factor Rāmānuja was able to formulate a 'synthesis' of a different kind. In his vision of life in relationship with God, it is precisely the loving, trusting relationship with God, i.e., *bhakti*, which integrates and gives coherent meaning to the two other *mārgas* – *karma* and *jñāna*.

There are two important implications deriving from this:

(a) The soul's relating to God is not a mere *sādhana* aiming at some other greater end, such as *ātma-kaivalya* (self-aloneness, or sheer interiority); *bhakti becomes the sādhya, the end itself, the ultimate goal* which the *mumukṣu* (the one searching for ultimate liberation) seeks. For, there is in this vision of things, no greater good in human life than to be lovingly devoted to God, to serve him as a daily *kainkarya* ('what can I do?') to recognise and reflect on his goodness, greatness, glory and grace, to take trustful refuge in him as the perfect Goal of our existence.

(b) That *karma* and *jñāna* are integrated within the God-relationship also implies that Rāmānuja perceived human life in a *wholistic* way. *Mukti*, that ultimate release that is the true 'goal of human life', does not entail the denial of all other life-goals; rather they are enhanced by the God-dimension, in which there is also a search for 'liberation'. Thus, the renunciation of the *saṇnyāsi* (the ascetic renouncer) is not regarded as *essential* for the true knowledge of Brahman or for liberation through Brahman. And here again in both these aspects of his thought, we see how radically different is Rāmānuja's thought from that of Śañkara.

What is Mukti/Mokṣa (Liberation)?

4. This brings us to another important Vedantic question: What is the final liberation we seek? To some extent we have already answered this question. If *bhakti* is the ultimate goal of life, such *loving devotion alone* can put us on the road to *mukti*. For the being of a true *bhakta* will be based on the Lord's grace, to which we are to surrender and in which we find refuge. Thus, we come to recognise that all we have and all we do is in reality the Lord's. In this God-directed life every action will be free from any concern for self-benefit; such a God-lover will aim only to gladden the heart of God. In loving fellowship with God we are then able to share in God's infinite qualities, especially in God's perfect knowledge and bliss, i.e. *jñāna* and *ānanda*. Such a *bhakta* will certainly be on the road to the *mukti* desired.

Yet, *bhakti*-life on earth is seen by Rāmānuja as still but an incomplete preparation for life with God in his transcendent realm. We should not, therefore, said Rāmānuja, speak of *jīvan-mukti* (liberation in this life). The reality of karmic bondage still remains as long as we live within the body. So we are to wait patiently and confidently for our *videha-mukti* (freedom apart from bodily life); only then do we share fully in the liberating perfections of God. Then there will be such complete knowledge of God that all our finite limitations will be removed. Even then, though, it is as a *bhakta,* lovingly related but not absolutely identified with God, that *mukti* is to be anticipated. For the soul's individuality can never be wholly lost while it is in this *bhakti-mukti* relationship with the Lord.

Reconciling Differing Texts

5. This brings me to my fifth Vedāntic question: Is there some key-principle of integration by which a satisfactory 'synthesis' (*samanvaya*) can be effected, so that, for example, scripture's apparently contradictory *śākhas,* or strands, can be satisfactorily reconciled? Put it another way: how do we make a coherent meaning-system out of the great diversity of our phenomenal experience? For Śaṅkara the answer was simple: the identity experience of pure consciousness, pure *ātma-anubhūti,* provides this key, though it needs then to be supplemented with a secondary key, the principle of illusion, of *māyā* that leads to *avidyā* ('non-knowledge'). Thus, when Śaṅkara interprets scripture, he takes only the 'identity texts', the *aikya-vākyas*, as supremely important *mahā-vākyas* – all other scriptures are secondary and thus relatively unimportant. (To some extent a principle required also by Christian theologians; not all texts carry the same weight).

Then Śaṅkara goes further, by saying that when there is true self-realisation, there is no longer need for any scripture. Even the key-texts are understood as giving only a *lakṣaṇārtha,* an indirect, suggestive meaning. They can be but indirect hints pointing towards the transcendent Reality.

Rāmānuja, on the other hand, contended that *all scripture* should be taken into account as significant for our understanding of Reality. For, the key by which he interpreted scripture, just as it provided the key in the articulation of his *Viśiṣṭa-advaita* vision, was the *śarīra-śarīrī-bhāva*, the 'body-soul-realisation/meaning', i.e., understanding by way of the body-soul relationship. This becomes, for Ramanuja, the key which provides an intrinsic inclusiveness and which is inherently coherent precisely because it is an analogy deriving from experience of being both embodied in the world and yet transcendent to it. In the light of this key-concept, then, both texts which speak of the *oneness* of Brahman and universe of souls and material nature, and those texts which speak of his difference from all else, can be brought together coherently, and there is '*sarvam samanjasam*', 'all is brought together', to use the closing words of Śrī-Bhāṣya, Rāmānuja's 'Great Commentary'.

There are many other implications of this great analogical key, the *śarīra-śarīrī-bhāva*, some of which are explored in other chapters in this volume, especially the next essay.

The Ultimate Reality of the World and its Life

6. My final Vedantic question is this: What is the *value* of the world and therefore of human existence? Śaṅkara and the more transcendentalist Advaitins have no doubt about this: in comparison to Brahman's absolute reality, i.e., from the ultimate *pāramārthika* stand-point, this world is *mithyā*, false, ontologically ambiguous, relatively illusory and unreal. It only has value from an everyday *vyāvahārika* viewpoint, i.e., to the minds of those still in the state of *avidyā* or ignorance.

How radically different was Rāmānuja's vision of the world, even though he was well aware of the suffering and evil that accompanies embodied existence! Again, it is primarily because of his vision of the universe as the *body of God* that he finds both reality and value in it. Let me close with what I wrote as the conclusion to my chapter in *Studies in Rāmānuja,* the publication that came out of a Seminar held at Śrī-Perumbudur, Rāmānuja's birthplace.

> Rāmānuja's vision of Reality gives ultimate value to the cosmic process, and therefore to the *jīva*'s activity within it. For, this universe is the supreme Person's body and is therefore supremely real. But Rāmānuja takes us a step

> beyond this. The body, he asserts, exists for the sake of its self; its actions are directed towards the well-being of that self. Similarly, the universe exists for the sake of the supreme Self; it exists to serve and glorify Him. As his body, it is his *śeṣa,* existing 'essentially in subservience to another'. Such subservience is, however, no imposition, for the supreme Person is found to be a 'treasury of hosts of innumerable and immeasurably beautiful qualities, irreproachable, possessing an infinite supernal manifestation, an ocean of immeasurable and absolute goodness, beauty and love' (*Vedārtha Saṃgraha*, para. 142).

Far from diminishing human or cosmic value, therefore, this conviction that our service and our very existence is useful to the Highest Self, immeasurably enhances such value. In a strictly ontological sense, of course, Rāmānuja recognises that finite beings cannot contribute anything of value to, or anything that is needed by, that supremely Perfect Being. It is the Lord's graciousness that makes the devotee's *kainkarya* service acceptable. He is even ready to make himself dependent upon their loving service because of His love for them (*Gītā Bhāṣya*, 7-18, 8- 12).

What, then, is the final step in the soul's ethical progress? Surely it is to recognise that the whole universe (and especially human beings with their unique union of *cid-acit,* inner consciousness and the natural, physical world) is the Lord's beloved body. Just as the devotee seeks to serve the Lord himself, so he should seek to serve his Lord's self-manifestation in the form of his universal body. Perhaps it is this implicit aspect of the great *ācārya*'s core-vision (his all-determining analogy of the self-body relationship) that today needs to be explored more fully by his followers, and taken as the basis for relationships with others in God's body-world. In all religious communities we so often find a discrepancy between the ideals and hopes of faith, and the (often unseen) pressures of the cultural and political worlds in which we are enmeshed. This is the issue I intend to explore more fully in the next chapter.

2

Rāmānuja's Core-Teaching: The Body-Self Relationship

What first impressed me about Rāmānuja's teaching, was this Āchārya's frequent use of his *śarīra-śarīrī-bhāva* ('the realisation of body-embodied self'). Perceiving God as related to the universe in the same way as a *self relates to its body*, immediately struck me as an important analogical insight, not only within the Vedāntic framework, but for wider theological thought also. As early as the 1950s I made a commitment to explore as fully as possible the role of this concept in Rāmānuja's Viśiṣṭādvaita system.

There were, of course, a number of precedents for the use of the self-body analogy in describing the God-world relationship. It occurs in certain Upaniṣads: it was, for example, a dominant idea in the *Antaryāmin-Brāhmaṇa* of Bṛhadāraṇyaka Upanisad. We find it taking quite an important role in the Bhagavad Gītā. In earlier writings I have suggested that this source may have influenced Rāmānuja's thought more than any other (*E.g. God and the Universe in the Vedantic Theology of Ramanuja*, chapt.4). Other possible sources are: Viṣṇu-Purāṇa, the Tamil Āḻvār-poets, Yamuna and other 'remembered' writings. Despite such long-established usage of the *śarīra-śarīrī-bhāva*, it is clear that only

Rāmānuja took it as a *definitive* doctrine, the *key* by which to unlock the cosmic mystery.

Vedānta's main concern is, as we saw, *Brahma-jijñāsa*, the 'enquiry into the nature of the supreme Being', the Ultimate Cause, the Reality of all realities. Such a quest obviously takes as a central issue the manner in which this Infinite Being relates to finite, contingent beings. And this implies a consuming interest in the nature and destiny of those finite beings with which Brahman has this mysterious relationship.

The Upaniṣadic model taken by all Vedantins as the basic clue for their understanding of such universal reality is that of the *Ātman*, the Self. Knowledge of the *inner self* in some sense (and this is where the various schools diverge) leads to knowledge of the universal Brahman, so that 'all things become known'. While Śañkara understood *Ātman* ultimately in terms of pure *Consciousness*, and Madhva was to emphasise the idea of sheer *Will*, Rāmānuja sought to bring out the Self's *relational* dimension. Just as that individual self relates to a body (in a variety of forms), so the supreme Self relates to the universe, which is like a body to that Self.

In a key Upaniṣadic passage, the *Sad-vidyā* ('knowledge of true Being') of Chāndogya, the seer asks: 'What is the Essence of this changing universe? What is the immanent Cause of all its finite creatures? How do all become known by knowing this One?' The answer, repeated nine times, is: 'He is *Ātmā* (self); That thou art' (Chānd. 6, 8, 7, etc). Early in his systematic treatise, *Vedārtha-Saṃgraha*, Rāmānuja offers an exposition of this *Sad-vidyā*. Almost at the outset he introduces us to his key-doctrine: 'It is by knowing Brahman whose body comprises all sentient and insentient beings in their causal, subtle state, that the whole effected world becomes known'. But this is merely laying the foundation stone of his system. It is to the 'body-embodied-realisation' that Rāmānuja turns later (as we saw) in *Vedārtha-Saṃgraha* ('Summary of Vedānta') and frequently in *Śrī-Bhāṣya.* Though not right at the beginning of his commentary, he turns to it especially when in crucial debate with other schools of thought and thus when he wishes to delineate his own position clearly.

There are seven significant assertions that Rāmānuja is able to make by means of his self-body analogy:

The 'Inseparable Relationship'

(1) There is an *inseparable relationship* (*apṛthak-siddhi-sambandha*) between Brahman and all other beings. This relational view of Rāmānuja's holds throughout his system: in ontology, epistemology, cosmology, soteriology. One of his first arguments against Advaita is that all Vedāntically acceptable ways of knowing (i.e. the *pramāṇas*) are based on this *relational* understanding of the structure of knowledge. *Śabda* ('voice', 'sound', usually translated 'testimony') has no power to denote absolute non-difference, because language structure is essentially relational, involving words, parts of speech and meaning. *Perception* necessarily includes a perceiving subject and a perceived object which is distinguishable by certain features that mark it off from other objects. Inference too, being based on perception and other means of knowledge, can have validity only with regard to objects characterised by difference. In the knowing process, therefore, how things relate to each other is all-important.

Now, Rāmānuja's principal concern in all this is to establish a logical basis for theistic experience and belief. This belief takes as axiomatic that the Lord of innumerable glorious attributes is distinct from all other beings. He is to be worshipped and adored. Devotion towards this Lord is religion's essence as far as the theist is concerned. And there is little doubt that this *theistic* perspective was an essential element in Vedāntic tradition throughout much of its formative period, at least since the time of the great theistic Upaniṣads and the Bhagavad Gītā.

Rāmānuja, however, was unable to accept any theism that ontologically separated God from other beings. There is, he contended in the true Vedāntic manner, an inclusive continuity between infinite Brahman and the finite world of *cit* and *acit* – conscious and unconscious beings; these three forming the *tattva-traya* (the three essential entities). Such inseparability implies a *dynamic communication of being* between these three, similar to that between soul and body. Thus, Rāmānuja rejected any theism in which the universe was not seen as derived from the substantial being of Brahman, or any system in which the Lord is to be meditated on as quite different from the inner self. Brahman is *upādāna* (substantial ground-cause) as well as *nimitta-kāraṇa* (efficient cause). Even so, the basis for the God-world inseparability is not an innate similarity. It is rather because the supreme Self imparts his Being to all beings. They are utterly dependent upon the supreme One and his causal power.

This is what Rāmānuja means by speaking of the soul as an *aṃśa* (part) of the great *Aṃśin*. It is not a quantifiable *khaṇḍa*-part of Brahman; but it does partake of the very being and character of Brahman. It is a *prakāra* of the great *Prakārin*, not in the sense of being a modified aspect of Brahman, but because as an 'ectype' of Brahman, its whole character is typified by and derived from that Original. Such dependency and typification is most clearly seen in the self-body relationship.

The Ultimate Distinction: God and All Else

(2) The self-body analogy also signifies an *ultimate distinction* between the supreme Self and all other beings. Herein lies the importance of the name *Viśiṣṭa-advaita*, or 'Non-duality which is comprised of distinctions'. In other words, the nature of the oneness of reality is determined by the distinctions within that oneness. In particular, it is the Lord who is the Distinctive One, for his innumerable and glorious attributes distinguish him from all other entities.

It is principally because of the unique *otherness* of the supreme Person that Rāmānuja was unable to accept inferential argument (*anumāna*) – as did some thinkers of the time - as a valid means of establishing his existence or his character. Another reason, of course, would be the Vedāntic assertion that *scripture (Śruti) alone reveals Brahman*, and that all logical argumentation will in the last analysis be tinged with uncertainty.

This does not mean, however, that Rāmānuja could allow no place for an analogical approach to the ultimate mystery – hence his self-body analogy. His explanation of the name 'Brahman' is of some relevance in this context. This word can signify any 'great being'. But it is only to the *supreme Person*, the Highest Brahman, that greatness in its most perfect form can be attributed. Similarly, all finite greatness or perfections are found in this supreme Person to a supereminent degree. His transcendent greatness is not that of unrecognisable otherness. Rāmānuja accepts that there are analogical relationships between finite forms and the Infinitude of Brahman; hence his contention that all words refer to Brahman, the Inner Self of all, in their most ultimate significance.

This is very different from Śañkara's teaching that words have to be taken only as 'indirectly descriptive' (*lakṣaṇa-artha*) of Brahman. This *lakṣaṇa*-method was necessary to Śañkara because of his insistence that Brahman's transcendent nature is one of sheer Identity or pure Consciousness in which all verbal descriptions also have, eventually, to be utterly transcended, coming as they do from the world of finite forms and categories of difference. For Rāmānuja this position was quite untenable, as it blasphemously blurred the *sa-viśiṣṭa,* or necessarily 'distinctive' character of Brahman. He alone is the *Puruṣa-uttama* (supreme Person), while all other beings derive from his being, and point to his being.

If, then, Rāmānuja saw such inclusive continuity of being, why did he not also admit the inferential argument as a valid way of knowing Brahman? From our knowledge of beings that point to Brahman in their ultimate reference, why can we not think our way to the knowledge of the Being which is their source and goal? 'No', says the Āchārya, 'while we cannot say that there is no similarity of character, or that finite beings share nothing in common with their infinite Source, it is not possible to *infer* that Brahman is such-and-such on the basis of their similarity'. His transcendent greatness, however closely linked to his immanental control, must be upheld. All finite beings are as distinct from that supreme Person as the body is from its soul, in spite of their 'inseparability'.

The Reality of the Universe

(3) The self-body analogy also provided Rāmānuja with a metaphysical basis for claiming the absolute *reality of the universe*. Not for him Śañkara's distinction between *Pāramārthika*-level ultimate reality and the relative, merely practical, reality at the *vyāvahārika*-level (Indeed, while those two levels may have been intended by Śañkara primarily as epistemological distinctions, or different ways of looking at things, is this a threat to the very oneness of being he hoped to uphold?). Rāmānuja was content to allow the Upaniṣadic principle that the supreme Being is *satyasya-satya*, 'Truth of all truths', 'Reality of all realities', that Being by which all other beings can be known. But, far from diminishing the reality of those dependent beings, Rāmānuja held that Brahman's supremacy as their *inner Self* ensured their complete realness. The 'body' is real, because it participates in the reality of the Self.

Thus, for Rāmānuja, the *māyā* which, according to the Gita (4.6) has brought the universe into existence is not some delusory power that distorts the real character of things. It is the mysterious, miraculous, magically wonderful power of the Creator, who changes the subtle, non-manifest form of his inseparably related being into that form of a manifest 'body' that is creation.

Underlying Rāmānuja's extensive seven-fold critique (the *sapta anupapatti*, i.e., his critique of a major tenet of Advaita, found in *Śrī-Bhāṣya,* his major commentary on the *Brahma-Sūtras*) we find two important convictions: *Avidyā* (non-knowledge, ignorance) cannot be allowed to become an independent principle, for this threatens the sovereignty of the supreme Self. Nor can the universe be regarded as unreal (*mithyā, anṛta* – both being terms used by Śañkara), least of all from the point of view of the supreme Reality, for our universe comprises that Reality's 'body'. Its being is grounded in, controlled by, and given substantiality by its inner Self.

The same fundamental concern for the reality of embodied existence underlies Rāmānuja's contention that *mukti*, or ultimate release from *samsāra*'s endless cycle, is realised fully only when the soul is separated from its body. This is no Greek *soma-sema* ('body-prison') doctrine, for Rāmānuja held a remarkably positive attitude towards the body and its actions. Only for this reason can he say that God has the same relationship with the universe as a soul to its body. Even so, for Rāmānuja, material embodiment was a sure sign of the soul's bondage. His was the traditional view that such embodiment provides the soul with the opportunity to exhaust its karmic associations. Were the soul not subject to karmic law, embodiments would be unnecessary.

Even if this implies a certain tension in Rāmānuja's teaching, both the cause of embodiment, i.e. *karma*, and that which *karma* causes, i.e. embodiment, are to be taken as absolutely real. However exalting may be the experiences of Brahman possible to the soul while in the body, *jīvan-mukti* (liberation in this life) cannot be understood in an ultimate sense. Only *videha-mukti* (liberation beyond bodily life) can be taken as the final stage for which the soul is destined. Meanwhile, said Rāmānuja, the soul's pilgrimage in this world is quite real – still real even when wrongly perceived. For the world itself participates in the reality provided for it by its supreme Self.

Utter Dependence on God

(4) The self-body analogy also signifies the *eternal dependence* of all beings on the supreme Being. The theist Madhva gave even more prominence to this theme, by his classification of reality as two-fold, *svatantra* and *paratantra*. The Lord alone is said (by Madhva) to be self-determining, independent, self-existent. All other entities are 'other-determined', i.e., dependent on the Lord's will and power.

However, no less than Madhva, Rāmānuja was fully convinced that the whole universe is under the *controlling will* of the Lord. He is the *Antaryāmin* within all beings, 'the inner controlling Self whose body is the world'. Rāmānuja's definition of the body clearly indicates this conviction: *'yasya cetanasya yad-dravyam sarva-ātmanā svārthe niyantum, dhārayitum ca śakyam, tad-śeṣata-eka-svarūpam ca, tat-tasya śarīram'*. (Śrī-Bhāṣya 2.1.9: 'That thing which a conscious being is able to control and support for its own ends, and which is essentially subservient to that conscious being, is its body').

Included in this definition is another significant term by which Rāmānuja frequently describes the soul's character. By saying the body is a *śeṣa*, in relation to the self, its *śeṣin*, he makes the relationship a more personal one. The God-world, God-soul relationship has now become like that between Principal and subordinate, or Master and servant; the dependency is stressed just as much as with the *śarīra-śarīrī* and *prakāra-prakarī* analogies (The latter I have translated as 'ectype-prototype').

Indeed, Rāmānuja's final word in his *Vedārtha-Saṃgraha* is that the soul's essential character is to *serve* the Lord, to engage in a way of life based on *kainkarya* (a term derived from the servant's query, 'What am I to do?'). At this point also, we see a radical divergence between Rāmānuja's outlook and that of those whose spiritual position sees all *dependence* as a sign of lower-order existence: a dependent entity is subject to change and is therefore less than ultimately real. Not so, countered the theist; a person understands his most ultimate destiny only when he realises his dependency on the supreme Person. Failure to recognise this dependent character is the soul's real 'ignorance' from which it needs deliverance.

In the soul's surrendered or *prapatti*-life (which for Rāmānuja was simply the *bhakti*-life taken in its most mature form, and thus the *basis* for *bhakti*-life and not so much a separate *mārga* – see essays 5 and 9 below), the independent Lord makes himself so intimate with, so available to, his devotee, that it is as though he makes himself *dependent* upon that devotee (Bh. Gītā 7.18). Despite this intimacy, and the self-limitation the Lord thus seems to impose upon himself, in the last analysis the Lord alone is the Supporter (*ādhāra*) and Controller (*niyantṛ*) of every soul, of every finite entity. They are of no *prayojana* ('usefulness') to him, only in the sense that they are not ontologically necessary to his being. The Lord, though, is always necessary to their being, just as the self is necessary to the body.

God's Glorious Perfections

(5) The self-body analogy also helps Rāmānuja maintain the *immutable and glorious perfection* of the supreme Person. As traditionally expressed, the Vedāntic doctrine of *Brahma-pariṇāma* (the 'transforming of Brahman', in creation) does raise questions regarding the Creator's perfection. Because the Bheda-abheda school taught a direct *pariṇāma* of Brahman, Rāmānuja was even led to assert that their position is more dangerous than the Advaitin's. If our understanding of Brahman is to be ontologically satisfying and soteriologically effective, Rāmānuja insisted that an adequate view of *Brahman*'s transcendence to the cosmic process must be maintained.

Śañkara recognised clearly enough that the *Brahma-pariṇāma* doctrine needed qualifying seriously or Brahman is made subject to both the changes (*vikāra*) and the imperfections (*doṣa*) of the universe. But Śañkara took the extreme position that the whole 'modification' is an illusory process, certainly *not real in the sense that Brahman is real*. This distorting process, both epistomological and cosmological, is expressed by such terms as *avidyā, adhyāsa, māyā, mithyā* (ignorance, superimposition, illusion, delusion) and the *upādhī* doctrine with its similar meaning. From the viewpoint of ultimate reality there is no change, no actual process, no causal realism.

Rāmānuja offered a very simple but, to his followers, an effective solution to this Vedāntic dilemma. He contended that it is not Brahman's essential being (*svarūpa*) that is subject to the changing states of universal evolution; it is merely his *related* being, his 'body'. For, the essential Selfhood of Brahman transcends the mutable world, just as the self transcends the changes and sufferings experienced by its body. At the same time, these 'bodily' experiences are quite real even in relation to the transcending self.

Some critics, however, argued that if the universe is the *body* of God, then the supreme Self must suffer all its miseries and defects just as the individual suffers the pain he feels in his body. But this fails to take note of the Vedāntic and Gītā view of the transcendent character of the *ātman* in its inmost being. In fact, even in everyday experience we can distinguish between the inner core of our being and all the changing empirical states which that self experiences.

As John B. Carman pointed out in his pioneering study *The Theology of Rāmānuja; An Essay in Interreligious Understanding* (see bibliography), in the case of the supreme Person, Rāmānuja distinguishes between (a) his *svabhāva*, or inner distinctive nature seen in creating, sustaining, helping, loving and so on – i.e. God's nature in relation to other beings – and (b) his *svarūpa*, or Brahman's essential nature which exists quite independently of others. The attributes of this *essential* nature stand without reference to the Lord's *relational* existence, though their full significance will be realised only when the full range of its activities is taken into account. In any case, in all his divine attributes the Lord remains transcendent to the changes experienced in his 'body'.

So Rāmānuja concludes: 'The *pariṇāma* we teach does not ascribe imperfections to the supreme Brahman' (*Śrī-Bhāṣya* I, 4, 27). For, as he reiterates many times: The supreme Self 'is not touched by the imperfections and changes of his body'. It is by his 'incomparably excellent Lordship that *Puruṣottama* is able to create his universal body from subtle unmanifest state within his own being'.

This brings out the more positive aspect of the supreme Lord's perfections. As well as being devoid of all possible imperfections, his perfection is characterised by innumerable *kalyāṇa-guṇas*, his glorious attributes. There is his lordliness (*īśvaratva*), his profundity (*gambhīratva*), his generosity (*audarya*), his compassion (*kāruṇya*) and many more. Rāmānuja shows that he never lost sight either of the wonderfully *numinous* character of the heart of religious experience, or of the ultimate value of the way in which that numinous being is concerned for the finite world. This distinctive character of *Brahman* is essential to our understanding of his *pūrṇatva* (his 'fulness of being').

God's Accessibility

(6) The self-body relationship also implies the *gracious accessibility* of the supreme Lord. He is *sulabha* ('easily grasped/ reached'). As the inner Self of his universal body, and having a generous compassion towards all creatures in that universe, the Lord is always accessible to those who seek refuge in him. From the human point of view, given human inadequacies and the 'otherness' of the Lord, he does not seem to be *sulabha.* Every human action, far from resulting in the soul's release and its knowledge of Brahman, seems merely to bind that soul more firmly to the *karmic* consequences of its actions.

Rāmānuja, however, is able to bring the 'logic of divine grace' into the picture, making this an essential part of his scheme, just as it is in the Gītā. In general, Rāmānuja is quite happy to think of the soul's experiences as determined by the law of *karma,* for has not the Lord of *karma* introduced this principle of merit and demerit for the good of souls? Nor does Rāmānuja set up the operation of divine grace in opposition to the law of *karma* – however much some may see an inner contradiction here. For Rāmānuja, even this grace is normally available only to those who have prepared themselves for it by the prescribed means.

Rāmānuja does not tie his doctrine of divine grace as closely to the law of *karma* as some do, which would make grace available only to those who have earned it by their own effort and merit. Following the Gītā's lead, Rāmānuja sees, for example, the Lord's embodiment on earth as a gracious act that transcends even the deserving of his devotees. It is because of their *need* for him to be more accessible that he draws near in embodied form. In its original *aprākṛtika* super-natural form, the Lord's heavenly body is beyond the unaided reach even of his devotees. This heavenly Lord himself has determined to bridge the gap, and so an intimate relationship has become possible. On the devotee's part, determination to find refuge in the Lord is still required. But the basis of this refuge-taking, as of ultimate release, is the gracious accessibility of the Lord who is both the *upāya, or* means by which the soul reaches its destiny, and the *upeya*, or the final Goal the soul seeks. (In this we see great divergence with some positions in the great Six-Viewpoints of traditional Indian thinking).

Rāmānuja's interpretation of the Gītā's *Carama-śloka* (18.66) is relevant here. The text says that all *dharmas* are to be given up, and the Lord alone taken as refuge. Rāmānuja first comments that all religious methods are to be given up, though only in the sense that improper and selfish attitudes in performing such works, including *bhakti*, are to be renounced. The religious person should continually think that the Lord is the real agent in his actions, and should do them for the Lord's sake, realising that 'He is both the goal to be attained and the means to this'.

The second interpretation is based on the thought that a person setting out on the path of devotion (as Arjuna was) may feel that he is unfit for this, not having perfectly carried out the required expiatory rites. To such uncertainty the Lord says: 'In order to make a successful start to your way of devotion, surrender yourself to Me and make Me your refuge. Give up all anxiety about the required rites. For I am supremely merciful, the refuge of all without any consideration of their differences of birth and suchlike, and I am an ocean of parental affection for those who become dependent upon Me. I shall set you free from any such sins of yours'. Thus, the way of *prapatti,* of surrender, is integral to the way of *bhakti*; it is the Lord's *grace* which is the basis for the Lord's accessibility (All this is obviously pertinent to the long and contentious historical divide between Vada-galai and Ten-galai Vaiṣṇavas in South India).

The self-body relationship, therefore, is fully realised only in that dependent, surrendered, devoted, loving relationship made possible by the supreme Self. *Bhakti*, says Rāmānuja, is a 'special kind of love.... Then, as the object of absolute love, the supreme Brahman leads the soul to Himself', and the 'body' realises its inseparability from its Self.

The Value of Service

(7) Finally, the self-body analogy shows us the *serviceability of human life* in the divine purpose: the body is useful to the self. Rāmānuja points out that in this case the analogy has limitations,

for nothing can be of use (*prayojana*) to Brahman in the sense of being *necessary* to him, whereas the body is useful and necessary to the soul.

Yet, this does not mean that, according to Rāmānuja, the universe, along with human life, is without any purpose or value, as some scholars have claimed (e.g. R.C. Zaehner, Spalding Professor of Religions at Oxford in *At Sundry Times*). Rāmānuja's attitude is precisely the opposite, for he envisages an unusually positive value-role for all psycho-physical existence. Is it not the glorious *vaibhava* of the supreme Being? Does not the whole universe derive from his own related being, and thus comprise his embodied form? Are not all actions in the world to be done as a *kainkarya* service to him to glorify him?

On this basis, we find Rāmānuja arguing for a *karma-jñāna samuccaya* (a 'synthesis' of good deeds and true insight) though in a different way from previous Vedāntins such as Bhāskara and Mandana. Other Vedantins, including Śañkara, held that it is only *knowledge* that can lead to liberating oneness with *Brahman*, and even this is of the character of transcendent *anubhūti* (spiritual experience) and so is not knowledge as usually understood. By reinterpreting *jñāna* as *upāsana*, i.e. as intimate, worshipful, meditative devotion, Rāmānuja was also able to accept the *jñāna*-way as the ultimate means to release. But such a loving devotee, a *prema-bhakta*, will inevitably desire to serve the Object of devotion with his/her whole life, and with every action that is possible, knowing that this will please the supreme Self of all.

Thus, there is a *continuity* of knowledge and action, the two ways (*yogas*) being bound together by loving devotion, based on the supreme Person's gracious accessibility. In his love for his 'body', he even permits souls to act freely and responsibly, though they themselves come to realise that their inmost self is the Lord, the ultimate Agent in their lives. All this means that there are, in this self-body analogy, radical implications for our *social life*, perhaps far more than most followers of Rāmānuja have realised. If the whole universe is in reality the supreme Self's body, then each person we meet, indeed the whole natural world, is part of the divine 'body' of the Lord we seek to serve in our life. Should we not, then, serve all humanity as though serving the supreme Lord Himself?

3

Iconic Vision and World-View in Rāmānuja's Vedānta

Religious studies in India tend to be of two distinct kinds. There are those describing a particular religious tradition – its rituals, scriptures, doctrines, community life and so on. Then there are those writings, usually claiming to be purely 'philosophical', which aim to rise above all cultic considerations. Undoubtedly there is a valid place for philosophical writing, both by way of analysis and synthesis, that is not focussed on specific cultic traditions. Earlier Indian philosophical tradition, however is, directly or indirectly, *reflection springing out of cultic life*. The presuppositions underlying philosophical systems derive, even if indirectly and unconsciously, from deep-rooted cultic traditions.[1]

Vedānta's Ritual Background

In Vedānta especially, the integral relation of cult and doctrinal system can be seen quite clearly, yet is usually ignored in Vedāntic studies. The Upaniṣads, for example, make little sense apart from the background of Vedic ritual and spiritual practice. The very important Bṛhadāraṇyaka Upaniṣad begins with a meditation on the inner significance of the Aśva-medha (horse sacrifice). And the Māṇḍukya is a reflection on the meaning of that seminal *māntrika* utterance, *AUM.* Then the opening statement of that historic summary of Vedāntic thought, the Brahma-sūtras, is *athāto Brahma-jijñāsa* ('*Then*, therefore, enquiry into Brahman'). This makes clear that the *jñāna-kāṇḍa* ('knowledge-section') of Vedānta presupposes the *karma-kāṇḍa* ('action-section') as its antecedent. Even more clearly, after the Brahma-sūtras have dealt with the question of the nature of the supreme Being and the universe of souls and matter, we are led to think about the stages of life known as *āśramas,* as well as *pratīka* meditative practices, and so on – all issues arising from community and cultic life.

There seems to be a widespread fear that unless Indian philosophy can be shown to transcend and supersede all cultic influence, its validity is questionable. To attain universal validity, it is often assumed, there must be not the slightest taint of cultic or sectarian particularity. Thus, S. Radhakrishnan seeks to depict Śañkara's system of Advaita as 'pure philosophy,'[2] even though Śañkara himself says categorically that there can be no knowledge of the supreme Reality apart from the revelation of scripture – not a very promising starting point for 'pure philosophy'! And a relatively recent work on Rāmānuja[3] sees almost no influence from the Śrī-Vaiṣṇava Pāñcarātra cultic system in the formulation of his Viśiṣṭādvaita system; he is a *Vedic* thinker. Significantly, it is also argued that in some of his doctrines (notably his doctrine of the celestial form of the Lord, a doctrine to which I return later in this chapter) Rāmānuja allowed himself to be injudiciously influenced by 'anthropomorphic concepts', 'mythological fancies', 'sentimental expressions', and 'narrow orthodoxy.'[4] As a philosopher, it is argued, Rāmānuja should have been above such 'superstitions', even if there is scriptural basis for them.

Differing Stances of Śañkara and Rāmānuja

Of course, it has to be acknowledged that Śañkara did appear to sit very lightly to his particular sectarian tradition, whatever that may have been. We have to add this doubt regarding Śañkara's background, because although he is usually said to have been brought up in either a Śaiva or Śākta tradition, there are some passages in his writings where he gives every appearance of being a Vaiṣṇava.

This is obviously not true of Śaṅkara's position as a whole, in which all sectarian elements have but second-order ranking in relation to ultimate or *pāramārthika* reality. And even Rāmānuja's formal Vedantic writings do not give free expression to the Śrī-Vaiṣṇava cultic forms in which his daily temple and personal life was steeped. For the sake of Vedāntic recognition, no doubt, certain conventions in style and content had to be observed. But this in no sense means that Rāmānuja regarded cultic life as a lesser order of reality than the more abstruse articulation of Vedāntic ontology and epistemology. The very structure of his Vedānta indicates that just the opposite was the case. For, as we shall argue in this chapter, it was that cultic life which was a crucially creative factor in the formation of Rāmānuja's Vedāntic viewpoint, even though others will feel that such a position makes this a less universally valid Vedānta.

In fact, the very opposite can be argued: that Vedānta which incorporates an intrinsic *coherence* of cultic life and cosmological viewpoint, in which worship-experience and conceptual system are most effectively integrated, should be reckoned the most *authentic* form of Vedānta. For, surely, intrinsic coherence and comprehensiveness of vision are among the most important criteria for evaluating any system of Vedānta.[5]

Rāmānuja, then, exemplifies very clearly the intrinsic relationship between icon-worship and cosmic vision. The temple at Śrī-Rangam, with its central image of Lord Ranganātha, obviously played an important part in Rāmānuja's life as the great Ācārya of the Śrī-Vaiṣṇava community. He was also the Śrīkāryam of the temple, in which capacity he had to resolve a number of tensions that had developed in the supervising of the temple life. Despite the lack of many direct references in his writings to the Pāñcarātra ritual and literature, to the Divya-Prabandhams, etc., Rāmānuja most certainly continued the earlier policy of fusing the two great traditions, Vedic and Vaiṣṇava. Thus, the practice of more esoteric *pratīka* symbol-meditation as well as more usual ritual icon-worship (*vigraha-upacāra*) were essential in the cultic life for which Rāmānuja was responsible after Yamunācārya's death. There was, too, his personal devotion to his household icon, Śrī-Varadarāja, the deity of Rāmānuja's previous temple-home, Kañchipuram.

It is true that the Vaiṣṇava cultic tradition speaks of two levels at which the divine becomes present with his devotes, i.e. as *mūrta* (with icon form) and as *amūrta* (without icon). The latter are the *para, vyūha* and *antaryāmin* levels of divine existence and activities. Essential to sharing in these levels of the divine being, however, are the *vibhava (avatāra)* and *arcā (vigraha)* manifestations. Conversely, all the embodiments are intended to lead to a sharing in the unembodied forms, though in an inclusive way, for there is no intention of superseding the divine embodiments.

There are at least five ways in which we can see an integral relationship between iconic devotion (*upāsana*) and the understanding of reality seen in Rāmānuja's conceptual system, an inner coherence that would lead us to suppose that it is in this cultic life we have the creative springs of Rāmānuja *darśana*-vision. While such cultic derivation may be true of many other religious systems in India, in few is the cult-concept relationship so integral.

1. The Divine Embodiment on Earth

Temple cultic life revolves around the icon, with myths recounted and rituals performed in connection with it. Thus, the central image is the focal point of temple life, the most effective point of access to that tradition's sacred power, the place where that tradition's distinctive 'vision' (*darśana*) is most immediately manifest. Each temple tradition recounts the *sthala-purāṇa*, or the 'glorious story of that sacred place' (*mahātmya* of its *divya deśa*), that not only accounts for its 'greatness' in general for pilgrims, but confirms the glory of the divine embodiment in particular.

Clearly there was a shift of priestly practice, when we compare this with early Vedic religion, in which the altar, constructed for the sacrificial occasion, and the sacrifice offered upon it, formed the focal point of the sacred world. The sacred sacrificial fire, the embodiment of *Agni*, the 'house-priest' (though as *triloka* also related to the 'three worlds'), was probably the nearest counterpart of the later divine icon. Of course, not all scholars, including that great iconographer, T. A. Gopinatha Rao,[6] accept that Vedic religion was icon-less, though the evidence for this is strong: over the centuries considerable changes of iconic practice occurred. In any case, it is in iconic religion that the divine person is seen as most immediately accessible to the devotees. Hence, in Vaishnavism the icon is '*divya-mangala*', or divinely auspicious.

Closely linked with such iconic faith in Vaishnavism is *avatāra* faith (indeed, the image itself is thought of as an *avatāra*), the belief in special divine embodiments, again mythologically recounted, about which Rāmānuja says the following:

> The Lord of Lakshmi, he who is the opposite of everything that is evil...who is distinguished from all things other than himself... who is a vast ocean of countless auspicious qualities, each unbounded and unsurpassed, such as knowledge, strength, sovereignty, valour, power and glory that are of his own nature, whose divine form is a treasure-house of infinite qualities... such as brilliancy, grace, fragrance, tender softness, beauty and youthfulness... who is adorned with countless divine ornaments of various kinds... (He) while remaining in his own form was inaccessible through meditations, worship and such other (devotional) acts... Being a vast ocean of boundless mercy, affability, affection and generosity, he made his own form in conformity with the nature of the configuration of each of the several species of beings, without giving up his essential nature; and thus descending again and again into each of their regions... and under the pretext of removing the burden of the earth, (but really) for the purpose of becoming the object of refuge even to (unworthy) people like us, He descended to the earth and made himself visible to the eyes of all men... Having refreshed the entire universe with the nectar of his looks and words, pregnant with boundless compassion, friendliness and love; having made Akrūra, the garland-maker and such others the greatest of the godly through the manifestation of

> his surpassing beauty, affability and such other qualities... he promulgated the way of realising God through love, which is fostered by the ways of knowledge and works, which has himself for its Object and which is declared in the Vedānta as the means for the attainment of the emancipation of the soul, the highest of human ends.[7]

It is precisely this conviction that the transcendent Lord has *made himself accessible* to his devotees that informs Rāmānuja's whole Vedāntic viewpoint. As John Carman's study of Rāmānuja's thought has pointed out, *paratva* and *saulabhya,* supremacy and accessibility, are the two determining conceptual poles in Rāmānuja's system of thought.[8]

However much the details of iconic ritual may be missing from his Vedantic writings, it seems very probable that there was constant interaction of the experience of the *arcā* divine embodiment and the story of the *avatāra* divine embodiment. It is the doctrine of incarnation in its broadest sense, therefore, that is central in Rāmānuja's thought and which accounts for his continual emphasis on the Lord's accessibility. Even as we read his account of the surpassing beauty of the *Krishna-avatāra* in the above passage, we realise that Rāmānuja could just as well be describing the Lord's iconic embodiment; each provides the impulse for the other. Thus, on Bhagavad Gītā 4.11. he writes:

> It is not merely by incarnating myself in the form of gods, etc., that I give protection to those who seek refuge in me. I show grace 'in the same way' to whoever desires to find refuge in me 'in whatever way' they conceive of me and, according to their particular desire, take refuge in me, or resort to me. I show myself to them... (so that) they keep on experiencing my form, my essential nature, which is really beyond speech and thought even to yogis, experiencing it with their very eyes and other sense-organs in all the ways desired by them.[9]

There seems little doubt here that Rāmānuja has in mind the divine accessibility in the various iconic forms with whom devotees most normally seek refuge. For, this iconic form of divine embodiment is strikingly consistent with the *avatāra* stories.

2. The Universe as a Divine Embodiment

Far more openly expressed in Rāmānuja's Vedāntic writing is his doctrine of the universe as the great body of the Lord, a body to which he is the inner controlling Self (*śarīra-śarīrī-bhāva*).[10] This universal embodiment is the *macro*-cosmic aspect of Rāmānuja's vision of reality. There were of course numerous scriptural passages that Rāmānuja could turn to in confirmation of his self-body analogical understanding of the God-universe relationship. There was, for example, the important *Antaryāmin-Brāhmana*, and there were various passages in the Gītā, especially the statement repeated in numerous ways, in the all-important chapter 11, with its glorious *Viśva-rūpa-darśana*, (vision in the form of the universe): 'Behold the whole universe ... all unified in my body' (11.7 etc). But, in themselves these texts do not provide the key to Rāmānuja's system. A prior vision of reality had gripped Rāmānuja already and guided him to these texts instead of to others for his principle of interpretation.

Are we not justified in assuming that it was the practice of continual meditation, with its recollection of the Lord's nature that is 'like an unbroken flow of oil', that prompted this prior vision? It is one of the principles of both Upanishadic and Tantric meditation that one becomes as the object on which one meditates. It does not require any great psychological expertise to see that once the mind is concentrated on an objective image to the extent that inward consciousness is filled with that image, then this interiorised image is likely to determine one's vision of the whole outer universe. Conversely, the divine body upon which concentration is focused will be seen as including the whole objective universe.

Let me hasten to add that I am not putting forward this semi-psychological description as a positivist 'explanation' of the meditative process. The resulting 'vision' need not be less an ultimate revelation of the nature of reality. I merely wish to stress that Rāmānuja's primal vision, his key-doctrine of the whole universe being the body of the supreme self, coheres innately and consistently with the iconic *upāsana* that was so prominent in his cultic tradition.

3. Relationship as Central to our 'Knowing' and 'Being'

The 'realisation of body-embodiment' (*śarīra-śarīrī-bhāva*) in Rāmānuja's system is far more than a mere cosmological *metaphor*. It provides a fundamental model for understanding both the nature of reality and the ways in which we apprehend that reality. In other words, the organic and inseparable relationship (*apṛthak-sambandhana*) of body and self affords a comprehensive key for unlocking the ontological and epistemological mystery of our existence. As psycho-physical beings we are eternally in an inseparable relationship with the supreme Self; we are God's body.

At this point a pertinent counter-question can be asked. Why, in Rāmānuja's system, does the divine object of worship and meditation not so fill the consciousness of the worshipper (*upāsaka*) that subject and object become indistinguishably one? Why does Rāmānuja not advocate complete or *kevala*-advaita, as Śaṅkara did, rather than *viśiṣṭa*-advaita – that is, a 'non-duality determined by distinction'?

Why, in interpreting a passage such as Bhagavad Gītā 6.29-31, for example, which speaks of a meditating yogi 'seeing his self as existing in all beings and all beings in his self' – and speaks of the Lord likewise as being seen in all and all being seen in the Lord – why does Rāmānuja contend that in both cases the text affirms an essential 'similarity' (*sāmya*) rather than identity of being? Is it not because of his fundamental and continuing conviction that it is in the *relational* act of worshipful meditation that the soul is most surely in touch with reality, the reality of its own individual selfhood and the reality of the supreme Selfhood?

For Rāmānuja, therefore, the ultimate reality is disclosed in the proper relationship of these two, a *worshipping relationship that can never be superseded*. Hence, he can bring out the full force of the Lord's statement in this same passage: 'I am not lost to him, nor is he lost to me' (6.30). It means, says Rāmānuja, that the continuing reality of the relational mode of existence is assured because there is *similarity and not identity* between meditating souls and worshipped Lord, as they are 'within sight of' each other.

Early in his *Śrī-Bhāṣya* too, Rāmānuja had argued that there can be no valid knowledge, especially knowledge of the supreme Being, except by way of *relationship* (As we note in different contexts in other essays of this book). None of the accepted ways of knowing, i.e., the *pramāṇas*, whether scriptual testimony, perception, or inferential argument, can operate without the interaction of subject and object. Knowledge of that ultimate kind cannot supersede or utterly transcend the knowing process, i.e., the life of meditative worship that leads up to it. Transcendent End and means of its attainment must be commensurable. Thus, ultimate knowledge, argued Rāmānuja, or knowledge that liberates the soul, can never be pure consciousness as taught in Advaita. Consciousness must be regarded as the attribute of a knowing self; in the case of God-consciousness it means that by which the soul can cognise and participate in the Object of its worship.

What Rāmānuja also claimed was that within this mediated, relational process of knowing the supreme Self there is an *immediacy* of experience, a directness of perception, such as would be the case in the lover's knowledge of his beloved. Such immediacy is possible because it is the supreme Self who is found to be the inmost Self of all finite beings.

Corresponding to the *macro*-cosmic dimension of universal divine embodiment there are two *micro*-cosmic foci: the iconic embodiment mediating the vision of reality, and the finite self which is the knower of the Other, a finite self that is also 'inseparably related' to its body. In both foci the supreme all-present Self is the inmost Self, thus making an immediacy of experience possible within the relational life of meditative worship.

Yet, this immediacy of inner vision can never do away with the mediation of some kind of iconic meditation. And underlying the whole process of 'knowing the supreme Person', and intrinsic to that process, is a *relational* view of knowledge and of the reality to be known, a relationality that precludes any sheer identity of being or consciousness.

Some Indian scholars have claimed[11] that in this system of Rāmānuja's, epistemology determines the nature of ontology. While it is true that these two dimensions are remarkably well integrated in Rāmānuja's thought, what seems to be determinative is the key-vision of all things, a prior *darśana*, cohering in the supreme Self as body relates to its self. And integral to that originating vision is surely the iconic embodiment.

4. *Bhakti* in the Three 'Ways'

Rāmānuja frequently makes it quite clear where he stands in the ongoing debate about the inter-relationship of the three foremost ways of being religious – *karma, jñāna* and *bhakti*. The doing of action, he says, especially carrying out faithfully the duties prescribed in scripture, is of immense importance. To a limited extent, therefore, Rāmānuja was in agreement with the ritual-oriented Pūrva Mimāṃsa. He certainly disagreed with Śañkara's contention that the realised, liberated person has no further real concern with the doing of desirable action, ritual or social. With Śañkara, Rāmānuja was quite prepared to agree that liberation is not to be achieved by means of human effort, though appropriate action done in the right spirit helps to purify the mind and prepare it for the liberating experience.

What Rāmānuja also stressed (as we see in other essays in this collection) was that the person who loves God will delight in performing all good deeds as an *offering* to God, which in turn God also delights in. In other words, it is the *bhakti* attitude that makes all the difference in the performance of any kind of action.

And what of *jñāna*? Very early in *Śrī-Bhāṣya*, Rāmānuja makes it clear that he understands liberating knowledge to be adoring meditation on the great and good qualities of the supreme Person. The essence of such *upāsana*, as Rāmānuja sees it, is *bhakti* – trustful devotion, loving adoration, dependent sharing (*bhaj*) in the being and nature of the Object of meditation. In other words, it is *bhakti* that is able to integrate action and knowing, and that determines their role in this 'synthesis.'[12]

It is in the more esoterically devotional writings, the *Gadya-Traya*, especially in *Śrī-Ranga-Gadya*, that the more typically

Vaiṣṇava way of talking about the *bhakti* life is made explicit. The devotee is to delight in being the slave of the Lord, to see his whole life as one of *nitya-kainkarya*, constant service.

An incident in the life of Rāmānuja, when he was still being initiated into the Vaiṣṇava way, gives some indication of how this *kainkarya* attitude was first instilled in his mind. Just after Rāmānuja had broken from Yādava Prakāsh, his mother advised Rāmānuja to seek counsel from Tirukacci Nambi, a non-Brahmin disciple of the great Yamunāchārya. It is said that Tirukacci Nambi instructed Rāmānuja to carry a pot of water every morning from the well to the temple of Lord Varada and there offer it for the morning service to the icon of Varada. When Yamuna, near death, heard that Rāmānuja had broken with his previous teacher and was performing this lowly service in the temple, he sent for him to come to Śrī-Rangam. Presumably he recognised that here was a man whose acceptance of such lowly *sevā* showed his eminent suitability to be both spiritual leader and supervisor of the elaborate temple service at Śrī-Rangam. As it happens, he was also able to expound, in systematic doctrinal form, the ontological realities implicit in this cultic action.

Those who have written polemic against Hindu 'idol-worship' – and this includes a number of reformers and iconoclasts within the Hindu tradition – often ridicule what they see as the anthropomorphic idea of God being dependent upon human help. Why should the supreme Spirit need waking, bathing, feeding, garlanding, and so on? Yet, this is what is assumed by the *bhaktas* who perform the 14 ritual duties (*upacāras*) to that Supreme One in his icon form? It is certainly not for me to attempt a full-blown apologia for icon-worship. It may well be, however, that the idea of God's helpless dependence on his devotees' service is, theologically if not ontologically, nearer the truth than we realise, and that the dialectic of 'otherness-closeness' that Vaiṣṇava theology sees in the divine nature is most strikingly expressed in just such incongruous dependence by God upon human help. Rāmānuja at least was not afraid to say on behalf of the Lord: 'The support for my existence is under the control of those who lovingly know me (my *jñānīs*). Why is this so? Because the "one who knows" is not able in any way to sustain his soul without me. Therefore I cannot sustain my soul without him.'[13] Later, Rāmānuja speaks of the Lord treating those who have intense love for him as though they were his superiors.[14]

Picking up a similar sentiment, Pillai Lokācārya (Śrī-Vaiṣṇava theologian of a generation later) speaks specifically of the Lord in his icon-embodiment (*arcā-avatāra*) form as being 'dependent on the worshipper for all activities... (there is an) interchange of position as between owner and property. He appears as if ignorant, as weak and dependent.'[15] This has been commented on as follows:

> This is the peculiar privilege of the devotee when he can constrain the Lord of the Universe, as it were to dwell in a particular image.... This is the greatest grace of the Lord, that being free he becomes bound, being independent he becomes dependent for all his service on his devotee. In other incarnations of his, man belonged to God, but behold the supreme sacrifice of Īśvara: here the Almighty becomes the property of the devotee. He carries him about, fans him feeds him, plays with him – yea, the infinite has become finite, that the child-like soul may grasp, understand and love him.'[16]

In Rāmānuja's writings a much more persistent theme, of course, is the devotee's *utter dependence* upon the Lord, just as a body is dependent upon its controlling self. And this, too, fits coherently with Rāmānuja's faith in the enduring validity of turning to the Lord's presence in meditative worship. Ontologically it is the devotee, not the Lord, who is in need, and who acknowledges his need by turning to the great Self of all for 'refuge', throwing himself in *prapatti* at the feet of his Refuge who has graciously made himself accessible. Again, the term '*prapatti*' (meaning 'falling before' and is at the heart of the long and acrimonious divide between Ten-galai and Vaḍa-galai Vaiṣṇavas) is eminently suited to the iconic symbolism. Admittedly, Rāmānuja wrote very little about this *prapatti* aspect of the God-man relationship. But when human dependence upon the Lord's grace and accessibility has been made the basis of religion (as is very clear in all his writings), surely the only fitting attitude that should be the basis of all devotional acts is that of 'falling before the Lord', accepting one's status as a *prapanna*, such as is intended to accompany all icon-worship?

5. The Heavenly Form of the Glorious Lord

In Vaiṣṇava theology the temple is seen as a replica of heaven; it is *Bhū-Vaikuṇṭha* ('Heaven on earth') the sacred centre of the world, the focal point of the Lord's sovereign presence in the midst of the mundane. But we could well reverse this and suggest that the heavenly world is envisaged in terms of the temple experience, with the glorious Lord as the central figure in the heavenly court. Either way the icon is heavy with symbolism of the life of heaven.

The question of whether the Lord possesses a body, and the theological implications of this, frequently came up in Indian theistic debate. One well known argument was that it is quite incongruous to think of God as creator of the world (after the manner of potter or carpenter) for to create he would need a body to function with. And to possess a body would make God equally subject to the law of *karma*, and so on (See the next chapter for a closer look at such arguments).

Here, there is no need to go any further into this complex debate. What we may note, however, is that while most theists, Indian and western, have felt it necessary to affirm that God is without bodily form, Vaiṣṇava theology boldly asserts not only that the whole universe is related to God as his body, but also that he possesses a heavenly, supernatural body. Rāmānuja's emphasis on this eminently beautiful and supernal form certainly puts strikingly his rejection of the Advaitic view that all descriptions of the Supreme in terms of *nāma-rūpa* (name and form) are to be limited to the empirical realm for they are *not ultimately real*. Thus, Rāmānuja takes to the extreme his contention that God is essentially *sa-guṇa*, 'one with attributes', one who can only be understood as possessing innumerably distinctive qualities.

Other Indian faith-communities, however, while accepting this ultimately personal nature of the Lord, rejected the idea of his *super*-natural body. What Rāmānuja constantly emphasised is that the Lord's 'one permanent heavenly form is (entirely)' suited and appropriate to his being. Similarly,

> He has an infinite variety of superlatively glorious ornaments that are suited to his form, just as are his amazing weapons, his gracious consort, his infinite retinue of attendants, and his infinitely great realm manifesting his glory...(and his) celestial abode, the essential nature of which is beyond the grasp of thought or speech.[17]

Rāmānuja does not explicitly describe the Lord's celestial form as comprised of pure *śuddha-sattva* (pure being) as later Śrī-Vaiṣṇavas asserted. What he does claim is that the Lord's celestial form is wholly fitting to and integral with his eternal nature as supreme Lord of all. Thus, his heavenly body is as much part of his divine sovereignty as are his glorious *kalyāṇa-guṇas*, and this body is quite transcendent to all finite material bodies.

Even so, Rāmānuja's description of the Lord's transcendent body includes qualities of such a rich visual beauty, almost sensual in style, that are reminiscent of the visual, aesthetically pleasing beauty of many Vaiṣṇava icons. Indeed, the term 'beautiful' (the Lord's *saundaryam*) is one of the most frequent descriptive adjectives among the many that Rāmānuja uses. M. Yamunacharya described this 'ocean of beauty' as 'at once sensuous and spiritual... The physical eye that dwells on the beauty of God's image becomes the divine eye (*divya-cakṣus*).'[18]

If the experiences of the Āḻvārs earlier and other Vaiṣṇava Āchāryas later are indications of essential Vaiṣṇava traditions, then certainly it is this *arcā*-form of the Lord that captivated his devotees and evoked such ardent admiration of the divine beauty. For, these other writers are much more explicit about this than is Rāmānuja. It would seem that Rāmānuja's more cautious attitude in this matter reflects his very great concern – in his theological system at least – for the *paratva* (other) dimensions of the divine nature, perhaps even more than for his *saulabhya* (easily accessible) nature. Thus, Rāmānuja contended that only the supreme Person in his infinite perfection can be the proper Object of meditation when various *pratīkas* (foci for meditation) are employed as symbolic aids.

Can these icon-symbols then be thought of as carrying the essential nature of Brahman the supreme self? To this Rāmānuja replied that no absolute identify can be made. 'What is to be meditated on is the symbol only, not Brahman; Brahman enters into the meditation only as qualifying the way it is looked at...so that something that is (known as) not Brahman is looked at as if Brahman.'[19]

Rāmānuja here makes his position very clearly distinct from that of Śaṅkara. Looking at objects which are in themselves not the supreme self with a 'Brahman view' is very different, holds Rāmānuja, from taking such objects as in reality the one Self, but on which the objective image has been superimposed. (Continuing the above quotation) 'To view a superior person, a prince for example, as a servant, would be degrading to him; on the other hand, to view a servant as a prince would be exalting to the servant'. The ultimate Object in all meditation is to lead to the knowledge of his great qualities as supreme Person, and hence to the intimacy of *para-bhakti* or *sādhya-bhakti*, in which the devout, loving relationship is itself the End of worship.

It is interesting that Rāmānuja did not interpret the esoteric symbols (*pratīkas*) as *direct* representations of the supreme Person's presence, even though he is present in them as their inner Self. Later, this was precisely how Madhva, even with his more radical concern to stress the difference of the Lord from all else, did interpret these symbols.[20] Perhaps it was in order to make his position quite distinct from that of Śaṅkara that Rāmānuja overlooked an obvious opportunity to use his general hermeneutical key, the self-body analogy. Even so, his understanding of meditation and worship as mediating the immediacy of God-knowledge and God-experience is not negated.

The main contention of this paper has been that it is primarily the outer image which has influenced the development of inner viewpoints, and that Rāmānuja's system in particular shows the continuity of this process – revealing an intrinsic and very proper coherence of cultic practice and conceptual system. Yet, we also have to recognise that the influence has not been entirely one-way. As soon as religious people, however whole-hearted their devotion may be, become conscious of what is happening in their cultic practice and reflect on its meaning, an interaction of outer and inner images begins. Then, theology begins to determine inner consciousness as it participates in the very ritual action that first created that theology. When this cult-concept interaction takes place, it is the task of the systematiser (the theologian) to ensure the continued coherence of the two interacting factors. This Rāmānuja has done with remarkable perception and skill.

Endnotes

1. In *A. J. Appasamy and his Reading of Rāmānuja: A Comparative Study in Divine Embodiment,* Oxford Theology and Religion Monographs, 2016, Brian P. Dunn has stressed the crucial importance of recognising this 'embodying' background in interpreting theologians. It is gratifying to see his thesis begins with approving recognition of the importance of this strand in my earlier writing.
2. *Indian Philosophy*, Vol. II, London 1965, p. 445.
3. S. R. Bhatt, *Studies in Rāmānuja Vedānta*, New Delhi, 1975.
4. *Op. cit.* pp.53-5.
5. *Cf.* E. J. Lott, *Vedantic Approaches to God,* London & New York 1980, chapters 1, 3, 4, 11.
6. *Elements of Hindu Iconography*, Vol. I, Part I, p. 5.
7. *The Gītā-Bhāṣya of Rāmānuja*, translated into English by M. R. Sampath Kumaran, Madras 1959, pp. 1-4 (This quotation is but part of the remarkable outburst of adoration Rāmānuja gives at the outset of his Gītā-commentary).
8. J. B. Carman, *The Theology of Rāmānuja: An Essay in Interreligious Understanding*, New Haven & London, 1974.
9. See Sampatkumar's translation, op. cit. p. 119.
10. *Cf.* E. J. Lott, *God and the Universe in the Vedāntic Theology of Rāmānuja,* Madras 1976, *passim.*
11. *E.g.* A. Bhattacharya, *Studies in Post-Śaṅkara Dialectics*, Calcutta 1936, pp. 23-4; M. Sircar, *Comparative Studies in Vedantism,* Madras 1927, p. 3.
12. *Cf. Vedantic Approaches to God*, ch. 10.
13. *Gītā-Bhāṣya* 7, 18, cf. Sampath Kumaran p. 211.
14. *Op. cit.* 9.29.

15. *Tattva-Traya* III. 202, trans. by M. B. Narasimha Iyengar, Madras 1968, p. 27.
16. Quoted by M. Yamunacharya in *Viśiṣṭādvaita Philosophy and Religion*, edit.V.S. Raghavan, Madras 1974, p.208. This seems to be the commentary of Varavara Muni.
17. *Vedārtha-Saṃgraha*, para. 127.
18. *Loc.cit. Cf. Carman, op. cit.* chap. 13.
19. *Śrī-Bhāṣya* 4.1.4.
20. *Cf. Vedantic Approaches to God,* chap. 10.

4

Divine Grace in Indian Religious Life

An initial clarifying of what is meant by 'divine grace' will help our discussion. To speak of `grace' at all there should surely be some sense in which the soul is thought to need help or guidance from a source other than itself; and that this 'other' is 'graciously' disposed towards the needy one. There are, of course, other issues to clarify in seeking to know if it is in any way *meaningful* to speak of *iśvara-prasāda*, *bhagavad-anugraha*, etc. In other words, use of such terms as `divine grace' in any system cannot be taken in isolation from the total world-view of that system if its significance is to be understood. Indeed, is it not useful to evaluate the extent to which reference to divine grace (or any other such strand in a tradition) coheres with other aspects of that tradition? To what extent is it organically integrated into the total world-view?

The single most significant background concept against which to understand divine grace in Indian systems is the doctrine of *karma*. Paradoxically, it is this inexorable law of exact moral consequence, of action and reaction, that makes divine grace a felt necessity; it is even taken by some systems as the way in which the Lord expresses his compassion for souls, his concern for their eventual salvation, and yet for others is seen as problematic for a doctrine of divine grace. That it has been appealed to sometimes in community life as the reason for the lowly status of others is more than 'problematic', it is deplorable.

In general, Indian religious systems have held that the operation of karmic rule means that 'as a person desires and wills, so he does; and as he does, so he becomes' (*Bṛhadāraṇyaka Upan.* 2.4.5). Such an affirmation of the determining potency of the individual's intention and action is the single most crucial idea underlying the religious systems of India. Few attempted to expound a view of divine grace that was not basically *inclusive* of the karmic process, even if for others such a law poses certain dilemmas for the operation of grace.

We should note, though, that even in some forms of Mahāyāna or 'Great Vehicle' Buddhism the compassion, grace and merit of the Bodhisattva even become the *primary means* by which a person can break free from the fetters of karmic existence. Those, for example, who merely utter the name of Amitabha are guaranteed a place in his celestial realm, by virtue of the wealth of surplus merit he has acquired through his compassionate returns to earth for the sake of relieving the suffering of all creatures.

Even Theravada Buddhism, (or the Buddhist 'teaching of the elders'), begins with the confession, 'I go to the Buddha for refuge (*śaraṇam*), I go to the *sangha* (community of monks) for *śaraṇam*, I go to the *dharma* (the Buddha's teaching) for *śaraṇam*'. So, the Buddha's last words on earth are said to have been an exhortation to his followers to depend on their own efforts as the sole means of realising *nirvāṇa* – the 'extinguishing' of the flame of desire, the root of all misery.

The Buddha's 'Middle-Way' of enlightened living and meditating, being essentially more corporate than is the Jaina system, clearly has a built-in reference to factors outside the individual seeker, helping him on his way. There was, of course, the 'grace' of the *Tirthankaras* as a potent factor in guiding the soul, by their teaching, into the required way of purification. And, in Jaina meditation it is the ancient Teachers' images that are usually the focus of the aspirant's concentration; while, on the path to that goal various other focal points of devotion (even feminine *devīs*) provide temporary help.

I now attempt a brief survey of the positions taken by India's 'six-viewpoints' (*ṣaḍ-darśanas*) regarding divine grace, and I follow this with an analysis of some of the important issues.

The Ultimacy of Ritualism taught by the 'Previous Exegetes'

I. ***Pūrva-mīmāṃsā*** seems a rather strange phenomenon to the modern mind. It takes more seriously than any other tradition the ritual practice and propitiatory offerings to be made to the Vedic deities, yet it assumes that the deities themselves are insignificant ancillaries to the ritual system. The ritual action is thought to be so self-contained that each action has associated with it a transcendent, 'unprecedented' *apūrva* power that guarantees the desired fruition of that action, whether it be the joy of heaven or some earthly benefit that is desired. This seems to be a special application of the general law of the unseen potency of *karma*. Here karma's positive outworking, i.e., that beneficial results follow good deeds, is appealed to as the way for humans to realise their destiny. Divine grace has no place, though in later Pūrva-mīmāmsa it was said that the performance of actions enjoined in scripture is 'pleasing to the Lord', and the benefits resulting therefrom are the rewards the Lord grants.

Two Further 'Visionary' Positions

II. ***Vaiśeṣika*** and ***Sāṃkhya*** have very distinctive viewpoints regarding the nature of reality, yet on this question of the role of divine grace we can take them together. Both began as atheistic systems, and yet both accepted Nyāya's inferential method of reasoning, and in particular acknowledged that some transcendent agent is needed to explain both the initial movement as well as the teleological development of the creative atomic substances. Sāṃkhya accepted Yoga's practical method of detaching the self from the senses, from attachment to their objects, and from the distractions of mental activity, and so from all that is non-self, the natural sphere. Thus the mind is 'yoked' (the same verbal root as the now anglicised term 'yoga').

Eventually Sāṃkhya, along with the Yoga school or *darśana*, also acknowledged that *the Lord is a necessary focus* for the meditating self if it is to be truly liberated for Nature's seductions. In both Vaiśeṣika and Sāṃkhya, however, it would seem that independence of being is essential to the individual self's true nature and ultimate destiny. Dependence, even on divine grace, would distort this essential independence.

When we come to those systems – *Yoga*, *Nyāya*, *Vedānta* and *Śaiva Siddhānta* – traditions convinced of the existence, the lordship and the goodness of God, obviously the concept of divine grace takes on a more significant, even if not always a decisive role.

The System of Mind-Yoking

III. *Yoga*, as found in its exponents from Pātanjali onward, is confident enough of the reality of *Īśvara*, allowing an important place to him alongside of its two other eternally real entities: Self and Nature. Here, though, *Īśvara* seems to be a *Primus inter pares* (first among equals). To him are ascribed very great attributes, such as omnipotence, omniscience, eternal freedom, perfection of moral being, immutability, absolute detachment, ubiquity, bliss, and compassion. Yet, the Lord is never more than the *operational* cause, nor does he become the supreme *End* to be attained by the soul. He is rather the *means* by which the soul attains its essential state of *kaivalya*, the complete detachment from all that is non-self, and the perfect realisation of its essentially transcendent character, which is its supremely desirable End. Devotion to the Lord is an eminently useful means to this *kaivalya*-end, such devotion helping in the removal of all obstacles to mental concentration.

We should not minimise the positive features of Yoga's Lord, however. It is the Lord who establishes the dynamic relationship between *Puruṣa* and *Prakṛti*, adapting Nature's modifications to the moral needs of Selfhood, so that both enjoyment of Nature and eventual liberation from her seductions are possible. Some exponents have even said that the Lord guides the karmic process within Nature, so that they are useful to the soul's realisation of its ends. The Lord himself is said to be eternally fulfilled, eternally free from all object-motivated desire, so that all his guidance of the process results solely from *bhūta-anugraha*, his compassion for creatures. He has no *sva-prayojana*, no concern for self-gratification. Naturally he is thought to favour especially those seekers who are devoted to him, granting their desires, in particular their desire for the *kaivalya* state. Such devotion will also include the resignation of all actions and their fruits to the Lord. Meditation on his perfect freedom from such karmic attachment greatly helps the soul's search for its own freedom.

Grace, therefore, is a significant concept within the Yogic system, whatever limitations there may be to the Lord's ontological status.

The Reasoners

IV. *Nyāya* has a rather similar view of the Lord's creative activity: it is because of his *compassion for souls* that he creates the world (in this case by moving atomic elements) and that he determines the moral consequences of all activities. This moral governance of the Lord, in which he makes the universe a proper sphere for moral consequences (a moral governance exercised by his all-powerful will) is strongly emphasised by Nyāya as we would perhaps expect in such an avowedly rational system.

As in Yoga, however, God is not so integrally involved in the universal process as to be called its internal or substantial cause. His role is that of operating the process from without, transcending as he does the atoms, time, space, etc., though these are all co-eternal with him. Yet, the law of *karma* does derive from his merciful will and is directed by him in all its unimaginable complexity. This means his graciousness is manifest through the karmic process, and he allows himself to be limited by the laws of its working. Any other mode of operation would be arbitrary. Divine grace can never violate the destiny souls create for themselves. Thus he is said to be like a father towards his children, rewarding and punishing them with exact regard for their deserts. This eminently orderly view of divine grace is just what we would expect from the exponents of the Nyāya system; there is certainly no notion of unmerited intrusion into the experience of creatures because of his grace.

The 'End-Goal' of the Vedas

V. ***Vedānta*** provides us with a rather sharp divergence on this issue of the role of divine grace; the Advaitins and the committed Theists part company on the nature of grace, as they do in their understanding of the destiny of the soul and the means by which this goal is attained.

There are, however, certain necessarily common bases for all engaged in the Vedantic discipline, even if in Śaṅkara's system at least some of this common material is regarded as having merely *vyāvahārika* and not ultimate significance. Thus, such doctrines as the soul's bondage to karma, Brahman as both efficient and substantial cause, both means and end, his lordship and his incarnate activity, devotion to the Lord, and even the efficacy of his grace in the soul's search for freedom – all these doctrines necessarily find some place in each of the Vedāntic systems. The fact that the Bhagavad Gītā comprises one of Vedānta's three authoritative sources (*prasthāna-traya*) makes it necessary for the devotion-grace complex of ideas and experiences to find a place in any Vedāntic system; the Gītā is such an emphatically *bhakti*-based work in which divine grace is integral to the understanding of God and soul.

Then, too, each Vedāntic system accepts in a general way that the Lord's goodness operates according to *karmic* law – and here also the Gītā provides the pattern. As a general rule life-experiences are given by the Lord as recompense for a person's accumulated good and evil *karma*. This is thought to exemplify both the Lord's compassion for his creatures and his lordship over their destinies. For, it is the Lord's will that operates this karmic law. Even devotion can operate similarly, for does not the Gītā say, 'I treat men according to the way they approach me' (4.11).

At the same time, it is recognised that the *samsāric* or continual cycle of bodily existence resulting from *karma*'s operation is that which makes necessary special manifestations of the Lord's grace.

There is a cause-effect chain of experience in human existence, and only the Lord's grace can provide a way of release. Thus, for example, the Gītā in its 'final word' declares the ability and willingness of the Lord to break this causal chain and set free the devotee who takes refuge in him. Such transcendence of the strict law of just-recompense is typical in the ultimate experience of both kinds of Vedānta; both *bhakti*-oriented and *jñāna*-oriented ways of release presuppose some kind of intervention in the cause-effect process.

We shall now look briefly at the distinctive features of the three major Vedāntins – **Śañkara**, Rāmānuja and Madhva – as well as some aspects of Śaiva Siddhānta.

Śañkara' s Non-dualism

(a) ***Śañkara*** represents with great consistency a radical non-dualist position, though this 'consistency' means positing different levels of truth. There certainly are a few passages in which **Śañkara** describes the seeker's progress as dependent upon 'the grace of the Lord'. On Gītā 2.39, for example, **Śañkara** comments: 'You have to sever the bond of *karma* only by attaining that knowledge which is caused by the grace of the Lord (*Īśvara-prasāda*)'. Even concerning the attainment of the ultimate goal, **Śañkara** can say; 'Then by my grace you will obtain supreme peace and attain my supreme eternal abode' (18.62). Nor is this kind of language entirely restricted to the Gītā-commentary. In his *Brahma-Sūtra-Bhāṣya* 2.3.41 **Śañkara** writes : 'The state of bondage in which (the soul appears as both) agent and enjoyer is brought about through the permission of the Lord who is the highest Self, who is the superintendent of all actions, the witness residing in all beings, and the cause of all intelligence. So we must assume that final release is brought about through knowledge caused by the greatness of the Lord. Why? Because, as the Sūtra says, "scripture teaches that"'.

Here, however, we are introduced to ideas that necessarily weaken the role of divine grace, though at this point there are little more than clues that are spelt out elsewhere more fully. It is suggested that the soul's individuality and distinct status as 'agent and enjoyer' is *apparent* rather than ultimately real. But to what extent is the language of grace meaningful unless the soul can stand as a distinct agent in relation to the Lord? It can, of course, be used in a provisional sense, on the assumption that the Lord's grace is needed in the preliminary stages before the full enlightenment of the Self's oneness is experienced. **Śañkara** concludes his comment above by saying we must believe in the Lord's grace, 'because scripture says so'. While this might suggest a literalist approach, his principle of *lakṣaṇārtha* ('indirect pointer', or 'figurative meaning') as a mode of scriptural interpretation was quite the opposite. This meant that every verbal statement is to be purified of its normal and misleading associations, so that its *indirect* meaning can be found. It is by this that we can understand ultimate reality in its true form. Elsewhere **Śañkara** accepts scriptural statements that he would regard as non-transcendent, using them in a concessional and provisional sense. This seems to be one such instance of a concessional use, the grace-symbolism being used as a figure of speech.

Other instances of grace-statements in scripture **Śañkara** sometimes ignores, sometimes interprets in line with his advaitic viewpoint. When, for example, Kaṭha-Upaniṣad (1.2.20) declares that 'through *dhātuḥ-prasādāt* (the seeker) beholds the greatness of the Self', **Śañkara** interprets it as 'through the tranquillity of the senses' (rather than 'through the grace of the Founder/Creator'). Three verses later comes the well-known statement: 'This Self is not to be obtained by instruction, nor by intelligence, nor by much hearing. Whom he chooses, by him he is obtained. To him the Self reveals his own nature'. Here also **Śañkara** continues his 'non-dualist' interpretation in terms of the Self's manifestation to itself, which makes talk of 'choosing', 'obtaining', 'revealing' rather meaningless. A straight-forward grace-theology would be the more natural interpretation – though it has to be recognised that a central concern of this Upaniṣad is the search for the inner Self.

Even given the radical non-duality of **Śañkara**'s ultimate goal, in which spiritual progress is not due to some transcendent

Being other than the self, but is essentially a process of self-realisation – even given this goal of an inwardly transcendent experience of the oneness of the Self, some *initiating agent* still seems to be required, someone to set the process in motion, to guide the soul into the path of transcendent self-identity. But, for this initiating help Śañkara seems to refer more often to `the grace of the *Guru*'.

Here, we do have to recognise that 'grace of the Guru' and 'grace of the Lord' are not exclusive; they may sometimes be identical. And what **Śañkara** makes absolutely clear is that no possible action or effort by the soul can effect the ultimate release it seeks. The way of *jñāna* is radically transcendent to the way of *karma-yoga*. Thus, the End desired is quite incommensurate with results obtainable by any form of action. There is a sense, however, in which his transcendental outlook is instrinsically conducive to a grace-based system. What else can account for the dawning of such transcendent knowledge? Once the enlightenment has taken place, however, grace-concepts no longer have any role; all such dependent relationships are superseded in the ultimate independence of the one Selfhood.

Rāmānuja's 'Non-dualism with (internal) Distinctions'

(b) If **Śañkara**'s Kevala-advaita led him to play down some grace-oriented texts, ***Rāmānuja's*** Viśiṣṭa-advaita was able to allow exuberant expression to all such grace-themes. By way of illustration we may take his comment on Bhagavad Gītā 4.11; 'I am easily attained, for I am unable to bear separation from my devotee. This means that I myself choose him, and I myself grant him that fruition of his worship that results in his attaining me; I destroy all obstacles to this end, and I make myself very dear to him'. Significantly, Rāmānuja confirms this interpretation by quoting the Upaniṣadic text mentioned above: 'He whom (the Self) chooses, by him he is obtained'.

Like all Vaiṣṇava Vedāntins, Rāmānuja regarded the Lord's descents to and embodiments on earth as the supreme instances of his grace, of his concern for the welfare of his creatures, and of his determination to be accessible to his loving devotees in particular.

There are, of course, numerous passages in his *Gītā-Bhāṣya* where Rāmānuja faithfully reflects the Gītā's principle of just recompense – the karmic law that the soul receives just what it deserves. Even in the devotional relationship to a large extent this principle must hold. Thus: 'The meditating devotee receives the reward of meditation, that is ultimate release, which means attaining the supreme Person' (*Śrī-Bhāṣya* 3.2.37). Yet, that same devotional relationship also leads the devotee to realise that the end to be obtained, which is the gracious Lord himself, can never be earned by means of his devotion in itself. It is `a gift received from the supreme Person himself'.

The Gītā's 'Final Word'

The interpretation of the Gītā's *Carama-śloka* is also rather crucial to this issue: 'Give up all your *dharmas*', says Kṛṣṇa, 'and take refuge in me alone; I will set you free from your sins' (18.66). Rāmānuja suggests two interpretations: (i) What is to be renounced is not action as such, but the usual attitude accompanying action: it is doing away with the desire for benefits accruing therefrom, the idea that works are one's own, the notion that one is the independent agent of action. And such undesirable attitudes can accompany any kind of action, indeed any kind of yoga, whether *karma, jñāna* or *bhakti*. What is called for is a radically new approach to all action: the Lord is to be regarded as the great Agent, as the true Object of all worship, as the Goal to be attained and as the means to this goal. In other words, take the Lordship of God seriously in all your doings.

(ii) Then Arjuna may have been depressed by the thought that he was not fit to set out on the path of this kind of devotion. In this case he is told, as we saw earlier, that the expiatory rites required in order to be fit to approach the Lord can all be given up (These purifying rites are perhaps the *dharmas* mentioned here, according to this second interpretation of Rāmānuja's). 'In order to make a successful start to your new way of devotion, surrender yourself and find refuge in me alone; for I am supremely merciful, the refuge of all without any regard for differences of birth and so on, and I am an ocean of parental affection for those who become dependent upon me. I shall set you free from your sins which are an obstacle to your starting on the way of devotion.'

Different Positions among Rāmānuja's Followers

Rāmānuja's followers, as is well known, are divided in their variant emphases on two modes of operation of the Lord's grace. These grace-methods have been characterised as *Mārkaṭa-nyāya* (as the monkey's young clings to its mother and thus is carried along), and *Mārjāra-nyāya* (as the cat picks up its young and carries it). The Vadagalais (the northern Tamilnadu sect) with their greater emphasis on human responsibility and the discipline of the devotional tradition, espouse the *monkey*-method. The Tengalais (the 'southern' group) emphasised divine sovereignty, the unconditional character of divine grace, and the invariable necessity for utter surrender to the Lord – and even this not in order to secure grace, but solely because such surrender is the only fitting attitude before the Lord. Thus, the Tengalais espouse the *cat*-method of salvation. While the Vadagalais also see no hope for salvation in the last resort except by the grace of the Lord, they claim that it will invariably be granted when this is occasioned by the appropriate condition of the human soul. The grace affording ultimate release is not sheerly *nir-hetuka*, without any kind of prompting cause, even though no soul can earn such grace.

Perhaps the decisive difference is that the Vadagalai sees even the *bhakti*-life as thoroughly informed already by the Lord's grace. For the Tengalai, *bhakti* itself largely involves human effort; surrender alone is the appropriate attitude before the sovereign grace of the transcendent Lord who even delights in the soul's imperfections, for do they not draw out and further enhance that grace? To the Tengalai, therefore, surrender is invariably necessary as the first and the last resort of the soul. And such *prapatti* is quite unqualified, being beyond the range of any possible preparation by the seeker after the Lord's gift of release. Moreover, so efficacious is the Lord's grace that once atonement is made, no further acts of atonement are required. Clearly, the Śrī-Vaiṣṇava schism is not based solely on frivolous issues, even though it has, no doubt, been aggravated by a number of sociological factors. The matters mentioned above, though, are crucial to any serious theology of grace.

Madhva's Emphatic Differentiating

(c) In moving on to consider the thought of ***Madhva***, initially we may note that he was the first of the Vedāntins explicitly to make divine grace a central concept at the outset in his Brahma-sūtra commentary. Having opened with an impressive eulogy on 'Narayana who is exalted in every kind of excellent quality', he goes on to interpret the initial 'therefore' of the first Sūtra as a reference to 'the grace of the all-pervading Lord'. The enquiry into Brahman is possible, he argues, because of divine grace, and it is 'only by means of his perfect grace that the soul attains release'.

This grace-emphasis in Madhva's system was an inevitable corollary of his constant emphasis on the Lord as the sole '*Sva-tantra*' or self-determining, independent Being. All other beings are (*para-tantra*) – they are dependent on and determined by the sovereign will of the Lord, the One with fullness of qualities (*guṇa-pūrṇa*). Even the veiling and binding of the soul is caused directly by the will of the Lord (as Saiva theology also stresses), so naturally only by the Lord's grace can the soul be enlightened and released. Indeed, the Lord's essential being is quite beyond the range of the soul's understanding: 'the light revealing him comes only through his grace....The glorious Lord is eternally unmanifest to normal perception (as all Vedantins would teach); but for the grace of this supreme Lord (to those) who long to see him, (who could draw near to) this immeasurable and almighty Being' (*Brahma-Sūtra-Bhāṣya* 3.2.25-7).

One way in which Madhva reinforces this view of the Lord's transcendent grace is by his doctrine of inherent characteristics, the *viśeṣas* that determine the nature, actions and destinies of each soul – thus preceding even the operation of *karma*. While it is the Lord himself who is the cause of these *viśeṣas*, they do make it possible to think of the out-working of the karmic law in a more dynamically personal manner.

Another concept stressed by Madhva is the *Bimba-pratibimba* ('Original-reflection') relationship of Lord and soul, an analogical idea more commonly found in Advaita than in theistic Vedānta. But whereas in Advaita the analogy is intended to express the transitory nature of the individual's ontological status, Madhva simply wanted to underline our utter dependence on the Lord and the Lord's unconditioned sovereignty in contrast to the soul. And it means that in Madhva's system the relation of souls (or cosmos) to the Lord is a far cry from the 'inseparability' of ontic existence posited by Rāmānuja's all-important self-body analogy for explicating the God-world relationship.

It is perhaps Madhva's ontology and cosmology that from time to time in his writing seems to threaten the very grace-theology he so strikingly highlighted, precisely because of his view of the radical contrast between Lord and world. This contrast was also expressed by denying that the Lord's being is the *upādāna* or substantial cause of the universe. It is the eternal substances such as Nature, Time and Space that comprise the world's substantial cause, he argued. There is, though, no doubting his intention to make the Lord intimately connected with all things by his 'entering into' them, 'pervading them' as their animating life-principle. In some passages, however, it is the Lord's *Śakti*, as in Śaiva Siddhānta, that provides this all-pervading immanental power. However this immanental dimension may be expressed, the very transcendence of divine Being that made grace so necessary, results in a certain loss of intimate inseparability even in the relationship of grace.

Devotion is, of course, of very great importance in Madhva's system. Sometimes he follows the Gītā's maxim, 'as men approach me, so I reward them'. Thus, Madhva can say that 'the Lord has to be moved to graciousness' by devotion. 'Devotion alone leads to the supreme Being, devotion alone shows him' (*BSB* 3.3.53). But this is qualified by calling it the Lord's independent response, though given 'in consideration of the soul's devotion'.

In most Vaiṣṇava theology, in fact, there is this continual interplay of devotion and grace, as also of knowledge and grace. Thus Madhva, for example, says: 'Without knowing him, the Lord's supreme grace cannot be obtained ... by knowledge only is the Lord's grace obtainable' (*BSB* 1.1.1). But he also writes:

'Direct knowledge of the supreme Lord can be gained only by his grace, not by any efforts of the soul' (*BSB* 3.2.22).

Then, in his interpretation of the Carama-śloka of the Gītā (18.66), Madhva claims that the devotee is to 'give up every activity that is not meant for the delight of the Lord'; he is to 'offer every activity for the acceptance of the Lord'. He recognises that 'even the possibility of renouncing other things wholly depends upon the grace of the Lord'. So, he 'rests upon the grace of the Lord'. He 'rests upon the Lord, not even a single act being done without feeling the grace of the Lord'. In this way the devotee bases his very existence on the supreme Lord's grace, so that he has a 'clear perception of the supremacy of the Lord, sets his mind on him, loves him above all other things, and offers everything to him..... This is the way of surrender to Viṣṇu, and leads to liberation'.

Whatever problems the outsider may have in integrating ontological and cosmological bases to this soteriological dimension, of Madhva's whole-hearted grace-theology there can be no doubt.

The Developed 'Doctrine of Śaivas'

(d) ***Śaiva-Siddhānta*** has been described (even by non-Śaivites) as 'primarily the exposition of a doctrine of grace'. Despite attempts to classify it as a form of Advaita, there is no doubt that Siddhānta's principal concerns are much nearer those of the Vaiṣṇava Vedāntins. Saivism does not accept the doctrine of *Avatāras*, yet clearly acknowledges that some principle of divine manifestation is essential to its grace-orientation. As the Śiva-Jñāna-Siddhiyar expresses this concern: 'Unless the Supreme can assume form, there cannot be a manifestation of grace to the devotee...' (1.54). Thus, while Siddhānta may speak of Śiva as essentially *Nirguṇa* ('without/beyond qualities'), its whole outlook is much more akin to the Vaiṣṇava emphasis that Brahman is ultimately *Saguṇa*. He is '*Nirguṇa*' only in the sense of lacking imperfections and not being exhaustively describable.

How then does Siddhānta describe the Lord? 'His form is grace, his attributes are grace, his functions arise from grace, his limbs are grace, and his grace is all for the sake of souls, not for himself' (*SJS* 1.47). All his five causal functions are said to be motivated solely by grace. Cosmic dissolution, for example, is said to afford a period of repose in their endless cycle of *samsāra*, hence is a gracious action.

In general, Siddhānta's causal theory is nearer to Madhva's than to any other system. The Lord is efficient or operating cause only. For Siddhānta his *Śakti* is the instrumental and *māyā* is the substantial cause in creation – 'māyā' here meaning that formless primordial Nature-principle similarly found in Madhva's system. But Siddhānta's three-fold division of ontic reality into *Pati, Paśu* and *Pāsam* (the Lord, his 'cattle', the binding cord) is in some respects nearer to Śrī-Vaiṣṇava's *Tattva-traya* (*Īśvara, cit, acit*) than to Madhva's five-fold classification of universal difference. The universe is even described as the *body* of the Lord, an analogy obviously all-important in Sri-Vaishnavism, and occasionally used in Madhva too, though clearly very differently from Rāmānuja.

The devotional path described by Siddhānta as leading the soul progressively nearer to the Lord is also rather similar to forms of Vaisnavism. There is *sālokya, sāmīpya, sārūpya*, and *sāyujya*, each suggesting a closer and more intimate relationship. Thus, various dynamic aspects of divine grace are classified as needed to create such forms of intimate relationship. Grace and *Śakti*, mythologically expressed as the Lord's Consort, are equated (Perhaps we should note in passing that in Vaiṣṇavism too the Lord's grace is sometimes said to operate through, perhaps only through, Śrī or Lakṣmi). Thus, it is said in Śiva-Jñāna-Siddhiyar that 'Grace is *Śakti*, and if there were no *Śakti*, Śiva himself cannot be manifest; and if there were no Śiva, there would be no *Śakti*'. In fact, throughout Siddhānta the Lord's grace is expressed in striking mythological symbolism. As the blue-throated Nīlakanṭa, as the moon-carrying Candraśekhar, as the mother-like 'Ear-ring-wearer', and so on, he is graphically depicted as constantly acting graciously, *even to the extent of self-negating suffering* for the sake of suffering souls, his beloved 'herd of cattle'.

In that the whole karmic process is the Lord's provision for the gradual salvation of souls fettered by that bond innate to a process that is part of the Lord's own body, there is no doubting the gracious character of the whole process as taught in Siddhānta. In this well-integrated system, a fundamental grace-orientation seems to be its principle of coherence.

Conclusion

A similar comment could be made of Madhva's theology in that divine grace is given such an immediately prominent place in his formal theological writing

Yet, while these are traditions in which a doctrine of grace is more dominant, it is Rāmānuja's theology, with its determining *self-body analogy*, that provides the most convincing cosmological undergirding for a *coherent* grace-theology. The inseparability of the relationship is fully expressed; the immediacy of the operation of grace is supported; the freedom, albeit limited and merely 'permitted', of souls is possible; the essentially 'personal' character of grace is confirmed; the supremacy of the Lord is suggested; the operation of the karmic process as God's expression of compassion is conceivable; the whole grace-relationship is necessarily real in an ultimate sense; and there is ample opportunity for grace to lead to greater experience of intimate relationship with the gracious Lord.[1]

Endnote

1. See my essays, 'Madhva's Theology of Transcendent Grace', in *Divine Grace and Human Response,* ed. C.M. Vadakekara, OSB 1981, and 'Grace in Karnataka's Madhva: A Meeting Point for Christian Theologians', in *God of All Grace*, a Festscrift to O.V. Jathanna, ed. Joseph George 2005. The issues discussed above are also dealt with in more detail in my earlier book, *Vedāntic Aproaches to God,* Macmillan, London 1980.

5

The Meaning of *Avatāra* in Indian Faith-Traditions: Rāmānuja's Realism

An area in religious studies requiring more extensive analysis is that of the relationship between theological formulations and the mythic/symbolic matrix in which they are grounded. (The issue is discussed from a rather different perspective in essay 3 above). Here the discussion is confined to some of the diverse ways in which a shared mythic symbol, *avatāra*, is placed in the conceptual frameworks worked out by the theologians of the Vedāntic tradition. Vedānta, along with related Śaiva-Siddhānta, is *the* great conceptually reflective Indian tradition to which a substantial number of religious thinkers are still committed.[1] Certainly no other Indian tradition has reflected systematically on the meaning of *avatāra*.

Reflecting on *Meaning*[1a]

'Meaning', of course, is not solely a matter of conceptual reflection. In the mythic imagery in which the *avatāra* concept is embedded, we have a rich seminal matrix for much Indian religious experience (broader than just the Hindu tradition). Thus, we touch the complex question of how theological systems relate to such mythic symbols. Is everything in our belief-systems equally symbolic, as some theologians would affirm? What is the process by which theological formulators find themselves with a particular perception of things that gives their inherited imagery one kind of coherent shape rather than another? Can we legitimately go further and ask (as this chapter suggests): Is one kind of theological shape not more authentic than another in the way it incorporates its received mythic symbols? Is one justified in suggesting that Rāmānuja's system in some way retains more of the intrinsic meaning of *avatāra* than others – allowing it a more conceptually determining role? Raising these questions should be sufficient for us to see the significant methodological implications that result from the way a concept like *avatāra* manifests itself in the Indian traditions.

'Descent' Implies a 'God-far, God-near' Theology

The word '*avatāra*' literally means 'descent'. To speak of a divine *descent* implies, on the one hand, a certain ontological *distance* between God - or the mythically expressed high locus of God's celestial abode – and the world, the place to which he 'descends'. On the other hand, the descent image also implies the possibility of a divine *sharing* in mundane existence. A 'God far, God near' theological dialectic (a Śrī-Vaiṣṇava phrase) is understood, although the precise nature – ontologically and soteriologically – of either the descent or the distance/nearness still requires conceptual elaboration if the meaning of this mythic image is to be articulated.

Just such drawing out conceptually is done, to a greater or lesser degree, by the Vedāntic systems. Other religious traditions, such as Śaiva Siddhānta, also affirm vigorously that God from time to time manifests himself on earth. Māṇikavācagar, for example, one of the foundational poet-saints of Siddhānta, eulogizes the accessibility of Śiva to his devotees, writing from his own experience of Śiva's special guru manifestations.[2] Saivism, however, never accepted a formal doctrine of *avatāras*, or of divine 'embodiment'. This is significant since it implies that in the mythic tradition generally, Śiva is less 'containable' than

Viṣṇu. In any case, in that embodiment, for Śaiva theology, means having to go through the *samsāric* process, it could not be applied to the 'Great Lord'.

Bhagavad Gītā a Seminal Source

There is no need to trace here the emergence and development of *avatāra*. Clearly the Bhagavad Gītā is a seminal source, although the Gītā itself does little more than affirm the coming of God to earth in each age, which he accomplishes by his mysterious power (*māyā*), coming primarily for the purpose of restoring cosmic *dharma*, or the righteous ordering of things, whenever this is threatened by the wicked.[3] In reality, therefore, Kṛṣṇa is the 'great Lord of the world', even though few recognise him as such. The disclosure of his divine character in the awe-inspiring theophany of the *viśva-rūpa-darśana* (the vision of Krishna as embodying the whole universe) was fittingly made to Arjuna because he was in a relationship of love and trust with Krishna.[4] Indeed, there are many passages in the Gītā, increasingly as it proceeds, which suggest an implicit causal relationship between *bhakti* and *avatāra* – an interrelationship, that is, between the purpose and efficacy in human experience of the divine descent and the attitude of love and trust. God comes to and helps those who love and trust him; and those who take him as their refuge, whoever they may be, will be freed from all the evil of their lives.

I do not deny that it is possible to discover an intrinsic coherence in the Gītā's conceptual structure, but for an elaboration of the doctrine (or rather doctrines) of *avatāra*, and for attempts to integrate it within a full-fledged metaphysical system, one needs to turn to the commentaries of the great Vedāntins. It is there that we find just how disparate are the conceptual frameworks within which this primal 'mythic story' can be placed. The hermeneutical setting becomes determinative of *avatāra's* meaning.

Convergence on Avatāra's Dharma-protecting Purpose

I shall examine the two most significant streams of both the more thoroughly nondualistic and realist-theistic Vedāntic interpretations, taking **Śaṅkara** and Madhusūdana Sarasvati as representative of the former, and Rāmānuja and Madhva as representative of the latter.[5] On a number of points, naturally, all are in basic agreement. As the Gītā explicitly affirms, all agree that the Lord has come to earth many times, in each age, both to establish *dharma* and in response to the needs of the virtuous and those who are devoted to him. That *avatāras* are repeated, Rāmānuja, for example, sees as evidence of God's *continuing compassion* for his specially beloved people.

On this question of the *purpose* of the 'becoming' of God there are obvious points of convergence, since the Gītā's text has to be reckoned with. **Śañkara**, for instance, at one level of evaluation agrees that the maintenance of social and cosmic dharma is necessary, and is one reason for the *avatāra* to 'prevent the occurrence of a void,'[6] as he puts it. Or in Rāmānuja's more positive words, 'to help the world at large, to relieve the world of its burden of evil.'[7] All these classic commentaries also see *avatāras* as in some way meeting the worship needs of the devout. The devotees' emulation of their Lord's way of life also has a place, for Kṛṣṇa said that just as he is ever working, his followers must work too, or the worlds will fall into ruins.[8] Thus all commentators find some revelatory intent in the *avatāras*, certainly in Kṛṣṇa, since the Gītā is a series of expositions of the 'mystery' of existence, culminating in the 'highest mystery,' when Kṛṣṇa as divine teacher reveals both his divine majesty and his divine love.[9]

There is another necessary point of convergence in the commentaries: the attempt to answer the question how the supreme Being can become embodied as part of the cycle of creaturely bondage. Does not all embodiment result from the relentless karmic process? How can God be subject to *karma*? It is precisely in responding to this problem of the *reality* of God's embodiment that one finds the most striking divergence between the Vedāntins.

Śañkara

I. (a) First, let us examine how the more radically non-dualist stream of Vedānta incorporated *avatāra* into its system, referring chiefly to **Śañkara** (788-820CE, though these are disputed dates) and by way of corroboration to Madhusūdana Sarasvati (16th-

17th centuries). For **Śaṅkara**, the *avatāra* is thought to function primarily at a didactic or revelatory level: it is a means of *enlightenment*. It reveals the truth lying behind the veil of illusion which obscures ultimate reality. Thus, taking his perceptual stance on the affirmation that oneness of being, oneness of the Self, is alone ultimately real, **Śaṅkara** takes Kṛṣṇa's 'embodiment' as an indicator of this nondual reality in which he is grounded. At a subordinate level, of course, Kṛṣṇa is seen as teaching that Arjuna is to emulate him in doing those works given him as his dharmic duty. It is by such works that the world's well-being is ensured. But, all actions – Kṛṣṇa's teaching again – are to be done with perfect detachment, without concern for their benefits. Thus will the bondage of *karma* be broken.

For **Śaṅkara**, however, there is a point of radical discontinuity between a life of action, leading to a lesser reality, and a life of renunciation, leading to an ultimately real level of being. Dharmic action may be useful in helping to purify the mind, but only the *abandoning* of all action can result in knowledge of the Ultimate.[10] Once the oneness of transcendent selfhood is realised, all worldly action has been superseded, although a few enlightened souls may wish to continue their life of action as an example, like Kṛṣṇa's, to a world still deluded.

The 'Descent' as Revelatory

The secret of Kṛṣṇa's ability to disclose the truth, Śaṅkara held, was that the vision was clear of that distorting veil of ignorance which obscures reality from other embodied beings. Kṛṣṇa, therefore, experiencing true 'Brahman-becoming', or the oneness of Selfhood, realised that his self (as all selves) is in reality 'eternal, pure, enlightened, and unbound.'[11] Free of the primal ignorance besetting other embodied beings, Kṛṣṇa was able to disclose the way of enlightenment to others. His embodiment, according to Śaṅkara's interpretation, exemplifies the truth beyond all embodiments. What was true with dramatic clarity of the divine embodiment is essentially true of every embodied self. There is but one ultimate Selfhood, one ultimate identity of Being.

At the moment of self-enlightenment, therefore, neither emulation of the way of Kṛṣṇa in his *avatāra*-life, nor faithfulness and receptiveness to his disclosure, nor any kind of relational attitude remains essential. Any such attitude of dependency is to be transposed to the way of direct self-realisation, the immediate vision of reality. Scriptures, *avatāras*, and *bhakti* relationships are superseded.

This means that there is an unresolved tension between *revelation* and *realisation* in Śañkara's elaboration of the Gītā, similar to the dialectic between the two levels of truth and being affirmed in his system. In advocating this doctrine, he was following the example of the two-levels theory of the Mahāyāna Buddhist, Nagarjuna. The 'everyday' empirical (*vyāvahārika*) level of existence is sharply distinguished from the ultimate (*pāramārthika*) level of true being. This is paralleled by a series of other dialectical distinctions: for example, between Brahman as *saguṇa*, one who is characterised by distinguishable qualities (at which level devotional love and trust are appropriate), and as *nirguṇa*, one who is beyond all qualifiable states (a level at which only immediately apprehended knowledge is appropriate); there is a distinction also between the duties necessary in social relationships and the pure-being possible to the self in knowledge.[12]

An 'As-if' Embodiment

Karṣṇ too, for Kṛṣṇa, seemed to share this dialectically opposed mode of existence. But 'seemed' must be taken seriously here, for Śañkara offers a radical way of resolving any dialectical tension in the divine descent. Kṛṣṇa was not a *real* embodiment of God's ultimate being, but was merely an 'as if' embodiment. In the Gītā itself, as noted above, Kṛṣṇa had declared that his *avatāra* is brought about by this mysterious power, his '*māyā*'; but there is no elaboration of just what this '*māyā*' means.

Śañkara initially interprets it as a 'supernatural' power, not bound by the processes of the causal chain of relationships found in the natural world. He quickly goes further, taking 'by my *māyā*' to mean that Kṛṣṇa was only 'as if' embodied; his body was but a veil of illusion. Thus, only the transcendentally enlightened are able to see the reality beyond, a reality with which in truth they are identical. Everyone for whom the veil of illusion has not been lifted remains deluded in thinking that Kṛṣṇa is truly a man upon the earth, similarly imagining that they too are distinct beings with particular bodies. Such people cannot perceive the 'unborn Lord, the ever-luminous... eternal, enlightened, free.'[13]

When Śaṅkara goes on to describe Kṛṣṇa's embodiment as effected from 'a part of himself,'[14] he seems to be moving to the language of realism. His meaning, however, parallels what he says elsewhere about the whole creative process: it is 'a part' of Brahman.[15] He interprets 'part-of-Brahman' language as not involving a real participation of creatures in the transcendent being of pure Selfhood, but rather in an 'as-if' sense again. The ultimate source of all being does not really become transformed into creaturely existence with all its finite limitations; Brahman only appears to be so transformed. Each individual soul is an 'as if' part of Brahman. Soteriology remains of a piece with ontology and cosmology in Śaṅkara's system.

Later nondualist commentators – at least those for whom *avatāra* is crucial – had some difficulty with Śaṅkara's interpretation. Does it mean that the *avatāra* is not a perfect vehicle of the truth, not fully revealing the Reality beyond? Not so, argued Ānandagiri. Śaṅkara intended 'with a part of himself' (God was embodied as Kṛṣṇa) to mean 'in an illusory form created by his own will'. And this interpretation is quite faithful to Śaṅkara's transcendental position, expressed less elliptically elsewhere in his writings.

Avatāra Points Beyond any Embodying 'Descent'

For Śaṅkara, then, any form of existence, other than the ultimately real immediacy of the Self in its undifferentiated state, is provisional in character, and in comparison to the ultimate Self is illusory. Even a divine embodiment, in distinction from the one true Being, is to that extent unreal. Its revelatory character is to be superseded by the realisation of true Selfhood. Up to that moment, however, for those still convinced of the reality of their own embodiment, the divine embodiment remains powerfully symbolic of true Selfhood beyond. The devotional attitude of love and trust towards the embodied Lord should develop into a consciousness of oneness with the Self beyond, in which there is no longer relationship but *identity* of being. The God-as-man, Creator-as-creature, Self-as-body symbolism, and the Lover-beloved symbolism it evokes, must be allowed to point beyond to the reality of the One.

Madhusūdana Sarasvati: Bhakti Affirmed, Real Embodiment Denied

(b) The extensive comment of Madhusūdana Sarasvati on the *avatāra* passage in the Bhagavad Gītā provides a significant supplement to Śaṅkara's extremely brief treatment of the passage. Madhusūdana was convinced that loving relationship (*bhakti*), rather than being superseded by the identity experience of true enlightenment, essentially merges into and *is* such identity. Thus, he is still a Śaṅkaran non-dualist, but allows much greater import to the Kṛṣṇa love-experience. For Madhusūdana, therefore, the Kṛṣṇa *avatāra*-event, in response to which Kṛṣṇa-love emerges, is of ultimate significance and is not to be superseded. Despite this, because Madhusūdana interprets *bhakti* and *avatāra* within a thoroughly nondualist framework, he too argues, and very emphatically, that Kṛṣṇa was *not in reality embodied.* Perhaps the added emphasis is precisely because there was greater tension in his system between the ultimacy of *avatāra-bhakti* and the identity of Brahman and Self. It is worth quoting Madhusūdana at some length:

> If there is to be a body of any kind, either gross or subtle, it has to be of an individual soul, a restricted and conditioned being, which God definitely is not. There is not a shadow of doubt, therefore, that God cannot have a body. Incarnation strikes at the very root of Vedāntic philosophy... God merely simulates embodiment... Such embodiment does not detract from the birthlessness, deathlessness and omnipotence of God... Vedānta has enviously been put under considerable strain to achieve conformity to the Gītā. The problem still remains unsolved. In the absence of a perceptible body, God

> may not be recognised as being in a particular human form. In his boundless grace he so wills that such recognition becomes possible by means of his *māyā*, his magical power. It is only an appearance and not reality.[16]

Madhusūdana goes on to a quote Śaṅkara approvingly that God 'appears as if with a body'. Referring to another school which teaches a 'real embodiment of that unfragmentable, immutable principle of bliss', he concludes that 'it is futile to discuss such a theory not based on reason.'[17]

Commenting on a later verse in the Gītā, Madhusūdana is even more adamant that 'the apparent birth of God is merely a sporting simulation of earthly existence... The enlightened know God's real nature... and realise that the birthless one is shamming birth for the welfare of the world.'[18] For Madhusūdana, then, the *avatāra* is thought of as of ultimate value, yet as an embodiment is also ultimately unreal; such are the restraints of the conceptual framework within which *avatāra* is interpreted. And in general, Madhusūdana's exposition of the Gītā is representative of the crucial Kṛṣṇa-bhakti movements of various parts of North India.

II. We now turn to those Vedāntins who see theistic experience, and the distinctions made within that experience between God and universe, as having ultimate reality. Here we have a very different conceptual world, though Madhusūdana was in agreement with the theistic view that *bhakti* is all-important, and there are significant differences between one theist and another. The conceptual patterns, therefore, should not be seen in terms of a simple division between nondualists and theists.

Rāmānuja

(a) The interpretation of *avatāra* given by Rāmānuja, despite the relatively restrained style of his *Bhāṣyas*, was primarily intended to draw out the intimate relationship that God, by means of his embodiment on earth, has established with his beloved devotees. He came as Kṛṣṇa because he was compassionately concerned to make himself more accessible to those who love and trust him. 'Being a vast ocean of boundless compassion, condescension, affection and generosity... he assumed bodily forms, overwhelmed by his affection for those who seek refuge in him.'[19]

Accessibility through an Embodiment of Captivating Beauty

Obviously, Rāmānuja was able to see other motives also: as is declared in the Gītā, God comes to earth to give help 'to those devoted loyally to *dharma* and to [God]'; the destruction of the evil that threatens *dharma* is of only secondary import. This fits Rāmānuja's emphasis on the newly established *accessibility* of God through his embodiment, which means that distinctions between people who seek refuge in God 'no longer enter into consideration.'[20] By manifesting himself in the beautiful form of Kṛṣṇa, God has captivated the hearts of all kinds of people. His beauty absorbs their minds so that their will becomes his will, and their desire is only to know him.[21]

This theme in Rāmānuja – the captivating *beauty* of God – merits further comment. It is usually the beauty of the divine form that is explicitly eulogized, and we can presume that it is the image-form of God – so central to Vaiṣṇava worship and in Vaiṣṇava writing often called another kind of *avatāra* – that is the focal point in Rāmānuja's perception of the divine beauty. As we saw in the third chapter above, there is good reason to think that iconic ritual plays a significant role in determining the kind of cosmic vision underlying developed conceptual systems such as Rāmānuja's. But this is not a one-way process, with theology acting merely as a projection of deeper perceptions inherent in ritual practise. There is, for example, a more complex interaction between the iconic vision and descriptions of either the beauty of God's supernatural, celestial form and his earthly *avatāra* form.[22]

The Total Reality of the Embodiment

More explicitly significant in Rāmānuja's theology of divine embodiment on earth is the seminal analogy which elsewhere I describe as the hermeneutic key to his system.[23] I refer to the self-body analogy by which Rāmānuja articulated the 'inseparable relationship', as well as the ultimate distinction, between God and his universe. The material world, in conjunction with sentient beings, comprises the 'body' of God, who is the 'inner Self', and 'inner controller' of all. It is this core vision (*darśana*), with its wide-ranging implications that must be seen as determinative of the meaning Rāmānuja attaches to so many other doctrines, including that of God's embodiment on earth in his special *avatāra* forms.

Concerning the theme mentioned earlier - that God's embodiment on earth results in his intimate accessibility - it should be noted (as we did in an earlier essay) that in commenting on the Gītā Rāmānuja even states that God becomes *dependent*, for the sustaining of his being, on the loving devotion of his devotees, just as they are dependent upon him.[24] However, in view of his repeated assertion that the whole universe is absolutely dependent upon God (as the body is dependent upon its soul), this should hardly be taken as ontologically definitive. It is rather a hyperbolic expression of the intimacy of the 'inseparable relationship' between the divine lover and his beloved. Rāmānuja is equally insistent that each soul, even at the culmination of devotional love, in some ways has a being that is distinct from God. He sees this *distinctiveness* (*viśiṣṭatva*) as necessary for the relationship to exist, and it is this *relational* existence that is ontologically ultimate. Such an ontology, especially as articulated in his self-body analogy, would seem to provide a more intrinsically appropriate framework in which to place a realist *avatāra* doctrine.

Rāmānuja's realism concerning *karma*, however, does introduce something of a dilemma. *Karma* was no special problem for **Śaṅkara** because all action (*karma*), and the bondage to the cycle of recurring births on earth which comes from action, can be explained as resulting solely from ignorance. Action and bondage are real only to the unenlightened. Rāmānuja, on the other hand, has to take seriously the traditional doctrine that embodiment is a consequence of real karmic bondage. It is so real, in fact, that Rāmānuja cannot even allow the possibility of release-in-life (*jīvan-mukti*). For the body, even though a real part of the divine 'body', is itself a sign of karmic bondage. Full release is possible only after death (*videha-mukti).*

Yet Rāmānuja is equally insistent that the embodiment of Kṛṣṇa is real, materially real. Thus, he takes Kṛṣṇa's saying that he 'had been born many times' as an indication that his embodiment is as real as Arjuna's own bodily life.[25] There is even the implication – perhaps dangerous in other ways to Rāmānuja's theology – that Kṛṣṇa has accepted a level of existence subject to karmic law and to the cycle of rebirth. Rāmānuja further explains God's embodiments as 'conforming to the different generic structures of various creatures.'[26] Divine embodiment is not illusory.

But Rāmānuja also asserts that *divine* embodiments are not subject to karmic law in the way in which all other embodiments are. There is no loss of essential God-nature in the *avatāra* life because God is the sovereign Lord of the karmic process, and is thus able to control *karma* for his own purposes. God comes to earth, therefore, 'without giving up all those characteristic qualities that belong to him as Lord of all.'[27] It is this mysterious, lordly control of the embodying process which is meant, Rāmānuja argues, when Kṛṣṇa claims 'by my *māyā* I become embodied on earth.' Even in his embodiments God's essentially transcendent nature is able to remain intact. In his move to accessibility and embodiedness he does not lose his otherness and immutable perfection. The *how* of such an act remains an inexplicable expression of divine *māyā*-power.

Avatāra Embodiment Corrresponding to *Pariṇāma* Creation

In Śañkara's system, illusory embodiment corresponds to illusory creation, and soteriology to cosmology. Similarly, Rāmānuja's *avatāra* doctrine corresponds precisely with his *pariṇāma* doctrine – that is, creation by God's modification of his own being. The mystery of creation, though, is that the transformation from unmanifest, uncreated being to manifest creation, with all its imperfections and evils, is a modification of only the 'body' or related being of God. There is no change in God's perfection or essential nature, according to Rāmānuja. Yet it is a real transformation within a real universe, because it participates in the reality of the universal Self. Here, too, it is through his miraculous *māyā*-power that God is able to effect such a creation.

Such a cosmological scheme provided Rāmānuja with an appropriate conceptual background for affirming: (i) the divine *avatāra* is similarly a manifestation of God's *māyā*-power, ultimately and equally real; and (ii) the divine *avatāra* expresses powerfully and mysteriously the accessibility of God to his loved ones – those who recognise that their essential nature is to be dependent upon him in an inseparable relationship, cosmic yet intimate. It is as a result of this special divine embodiment that the rich possibilities of the essential cosmic relationship become realised in Rāmānuja's system. For him it was the focal soteriological experience of the *avatāra* embodiment that confirmed the concept, arising from a more primal perception that the whole universe is an embodiment of the supreme Self.

Thus, one may tentatively say that while it is conceptual systems which provide basic mythic symbols with their interpretative framework (without which the symbols would remain hidden in the pre-reflective matrix of tradition), at the same time, as Rāmānuja's system confirms, intrinsic aspects of symbols can take a clearly determinative role in the formation of those conceptual systems.

However, in Rāmānuja's system, as in that of any other theologian, there is still a process of symbol selection that needs to be explained. Is there not a *prior vision of reality* that accounts for the selection of certain symbols rather than others, and that makes those symbols hermeneutically potent and conceptually determinative? Is it not also this prior vision that accounts for the essential difference between the systems of Śaṅkara and Rāmānuja, one seeing *avatāra* embodiment as no more than provisional and epistemologically symbolic, while the other views it as itself ultimately real? A similar and perhaps more important issue is why the *self*, the most basic symbol in Vedānta, is conceptualised so differently by the various Vedāntins.

Madhva

(b) The *avatāra* theology of Madhva also confirms the conclusions tentatively suggested above, although there are features of his system that add new dimensions to such a conclusion. Madhva was a theistic Vaiṣṇava whose thought overlaps with Rāmānuja's at numerous points. For example, Madhva was, like Rāmānuja, an ontological realist who saw the devotional life as ultimately real, as is the divine grace that is its basis.

Madhva's prior vision, however, gave crucial prominence to the eternal and essential difference between the independent, self-determining nature of God (*sva-tantra*) and the dependent, other-determined nature (*para-tantra*) of all other beings.[28] The sovereign, unfettered *will* of God is all-determining in Madhva's account of a real universe of life-beings, which apart from that integrating transcendent will would be a chaos of multiple and unrelated entities. Universal continuity is grounded in this all-sovereign, ever-fulfilled will. God wills to 'enter into' and 'control' every entity in the universe, without which the multiple primal substances that make up the universe – matter, souls, time, *karma*, etc. – would be eternally and ontologically distinct from God. They are dependent on him, yet are somehow quite separate from God's being.

It is this kind of theological position that provided Madhva with his primary principle for interpreting the divine *avatāra*. Inevitably it became necessary for him to account for divine embodiment as essentially different from other forms of embodiment. Thus, he laid great stress on Kṛṣṇa's being *free* from any karmic determination, for 'the very existence of *karma* and suchlike is dependent on the Lord.'[29] It is of great importance to Madhva, too, to affirm that there is no loss of the sovereign perfection of God's nature in his becoming embodied. His embodiments are special creations, described as unique 'manifestations' of the sovereign will.[30] While God makes use of material nature in his own embodiments, just as he does in creating the universe, his bodies are wonderfully free of those determining constituents characterising all other embodiments. God's *avatāra* bodies are not subject to such limitations.

On the other hand, God's embodiments are utterly real; they are not illusory as the nondualists argued. 'I came into being by my *māyā*' simply means 'out of my nature, under my lordly control.'[31] For, more explicitly than in other theologies, *māyā* equals *prakṛti* (nature) in Madhva's thought. There was not the slightest element of necessity in God's embodiments. Being free from all such karmic necessity means that God is freely able to create bodies exactly fitted to his specific purposes.[32] He uses nature supernaturally. Indeed, if he had wished, he could have both created the universe and effected the world's salvation without resorting to the use of material substances, such is his freedom.

Nor did God embody himself for any personal benefit. As other Vedāntins had affirmed, the world at large is benefited and God's devotees in particular. But Madhva picks up another Vedāntic image and uses it to refer more explicitly to God's freedom of *avatāra* action. *Avatāra* is merely God's playfulness (*līlā*),[33] a theme usually associated with God's creative activity. The idea here is that God does not need to satisfy some as yet unfulfilled desire either in creation or in incarnation. Rather, he acts spontaneously from within his own nature, subject to no pressure from without himself.

Thus, God remains transcendentally free, essentially unaffected in his inner nature by his embodiments in a world of change, pain, and sin. So great is his uninvolved freedom that Madhva even describes the embodiments as 'mere manifestations,'[34] or at least only manifestations of the supernatural body of God which has its abode in heaven, for that celestial body is in no way touched by the process of birth, growth, decay, and death. *Avatāras*, then, are seen as temporary but real 'manifestations', special creations which in no way subject God to the limitations of earthly existence.

Concluding Evaluation

So, in Madhva's account of *avatāra*, we again see how a shared mythic phenomenon takes on various shapes at the conceptual level, in line with different primal perceptions of the structure of existence. Some convergent features are shared by all these mainstream Vedantic interpretations, perhaps made necessary by loyalty to the common text. However, such shared features are seen far more clearly between theists on the one side, and Śankara-style non-dualists on the other. Both of the theists who were discussed belong to the Vaiṣṇava tradition, though to different branches.

Madhusūdana Sarasvati too was grounded in one of the *Krishna-bhakti* movements that derived from some form of theistic Vaishnavism. Thus, traditional roots are not everything. In Madhusūdana's case his primal perception derives from advaitic teaching outside his original grounding, although his continuing concern for the ultimacy of that earlier devotion-based faith certainly made some impact on his later conceptualizing. It did not, however, lead him to contradict the nondualist framework he adopted in order to affirm the reality of the divine embodiment or the relationship of loving devotion between devotees and embodied Lord. At this point the *avatāra*, for all its value, heuristic or intrinsic, must be interpreted by the nondualist as an ultimately illusory embodiment. It can never be more than essentially symbolic in character, and with direct experience of the Reality, the symbol fades away into the world of illusion and unreality.

Even among realist theists, as pointed out above, there may be other determining concepts, which arise from prior perceptions, placing considerable strain upon any concept of the *reality* of the divine embodiment. Madhva's determining vision of the transcendent Lord relating to the universe only through the utterly free exercise of his sovereign will, with its corollary that universal creative substances are eternally and ontologically different from God, pushes his conceptualization of the divine embodiment to the very edge of a realist interpretation. *Avatāra*, interpreted as real divine embodiment, finds only a precarious place within the kind of transcendentalist conceptualizing that emerges from Madhva's prior vision of reality, however committed in devotional life he may be to the reality of Krishna as the true *avatāra* of

God. Soteriological style is inevitably affected by ontological structures.

It is in Rāmānuja's system that we find the most appropriate ontology for a realist *avatāra* soteriology. For there seems to be an intrinsic correspondence between the hermeneutically determining self-body analogy, through which the universe and God are conceptualized, and the saving faith in the real embodiment of the supreme Self.

Whatever may be our evaluation of these diverse *avatāra* interpretations, it has become clear that the meaning this sacred story has for believers is dependent on the conceptual systems within which it is interpreted. No doubt a grounding in some mythic symbolism is essential to any viable theology, but even here there is preconceptual *vision*, from which certain kinds of conceptual structuring seem inevitably to spring.

Endnotes

1. It could be argued that, globally at least, far more people are committed to Yoga than to Vedānta. But Yoga is hardly a 'conceptually reflective' tradition of the same order as Vedānta. It is primarily a technique which can have several objectives and with which a diversity of conceptual systems can be associated.

1a. 'Meaning' as fundamental to theology of any kind is discussed more fully in my essay in *Hinduism in India: The Early Period*, edited by G. Bailey, series editor G.A. Oddie, Sage, New Delhi, 2017.

2. Cf. Māṇika Vācagar's *Tiruvacakam* 1.59-61; 'Thou cams't in grace, in this same earth dids't shine thy mighty feet.' Translation by G.U. Pope.

3. *Bhagavad Gītā* (henceforth *BG*) 4.6-8. A very recent and thorough treatment of the divine embodiment in the *Gītā* is I. Selvanayagam's *Kristu Bhakti and Krishna Bhakti* (New Delhi: Christian World Imprints, 2017).

4. *BG* 11.

5. Traditional dates for these four Vedantins are; Śaṅkara 788-820, Rāmānuja 1017-1137; Madhva 1238-1317; Madhusūdana 1540-1647.

6. *Bhagavad Gītā Bhāṣya* (of Śaṅkara, henceforth *BGB*) introduction. There is a translation by A.M. Sastry (Madras; Samata Books, 7th edition 1977, first edition 1897).

7. *Gītā-Bhāṣya* (of Rāmānuja, henceforth *GB*) introduction. There is a translation by M.R. Sampath Kumaran (Madras: Memorial Trust, 1969).

8. *BG* 3.23-4.

9. See esp. 18.63-4.

10. *Cf. BGB intro.* and *passim.*
11. See, e.g., *BGB*7.24, 9.11; *Brahma-Sūtra-Bhāṣya* 1.1.2, 1.1.4.
12. *Cf.* E.J. Lott, *Vedantic Approaches to God* (London: Macmillan, 1980), esp. chapters 5, 7, 8.
13. *BG* 4.6.
14. *BGB* introduction.
15. *Brahma-Sūtra-Bhāṣya* 2.3.42. Cf. BG 10.41-2: 'I stand sustaining this world with one part of myself.'
16. *Gūḍārtha-Dīpika* 4.6, translated as *Madhusūdana Sarasvati on Bhagavad Gītā,* by S.K. Gupta (Delhi: Motilal Banarsidass, 1977). For clarity I have slightly revised Gupta's language, though I confess I have not checked his translation with the original Sanskrit, as I have done with other Āchāryas here referred to.
17. *Ibid.*
18. *Ibid.* 4.9.
19. *GB* Introduction.
20. *GB* 6.47.
21. *GB* Introduction.
22. Cf. E.J. Lott, 'Iconic Vision and Cosmic Viewpoint in Rāmānuja's Vedānta', *Ananthacharya Indological Research Institute Series X,* ed. K.K.A. Venkatachari (Bombay: AIRI, 1981), 3046.
23. Cf. E.J. Lott, 'Rāmānuja's *Śarīra-Śarīrī-Bhāva*: A Conceptual Analysis,' in *Studies in Rāmānuja* (Madras: Rāmānuja Vedānta Centre, 1980), 21-40.
24. *GB* 7.18, 9.29.
25. *GB* 4.5.
26. *GB* Introduction.
27. *GB* 4.6.
28. *Brahma-Sūtra-Bhāṣya* (of Madhva) 1.2.8, 12; 1.4.23. Cf. E.J. Lott, *Vedantic Approaches,* esp. pp. 34-37, 56-65, 141-50; also 'The Fulness and Freedom of the supreme Lord: Madhva's Radical Theism,' *Bangalore Theological Forum,* vol. ix, no. 2, 1977, 42-60.
29. *Brahma-Sūtra-Bhāṣya* 2.1.37.
30. *Viṣṇu-Tattva-Nirṇaya* para. 453.
31. *BGD* (Madhva) 4.6.
32. *Ibid.*
33. *Ibid.* 4.8. *Cp. Brahma-Sūtras* 2.1.33.
34. *Viṣṇu-Tattva-Nirṇaya,* RGM 453, *na ca Īśvara-icchā.*

6

Interpreting an Upaniṣad from a Viśiṣṭādvaita Perspective

In the series of Śrī-Vaiṣṇava seminars in South India[1] which I shared from the 1970s onwards, in 1986 the chosen theme was an Upaniṣad, the Kaṭha. The 'contemporary significance' of this ancient scripture, especially for Vaiṣṇavas, was my allotted subject. In systematising Viśiṣṭādvaita, Rāmānuja gave great prominence to the tradition's *relational* vision of things – which he worked out in ontological and epistemological terms, as well as theologically and cosmologically, in explicit contra-distinction from the trans-relational view of *Advaita*. In recent years, however, it is *Advaita* which is assumed to be the authentic Indian way of looking at things, and Śaṅkara is rated – by scholars and by the general public – far higher than Rāmānuja. Although Bengali Vaishnavism has proved itself to be alive and flourishing, South Indian Viśiṣṭādvaita almost seems to have lost its earlier theological vigour, or at least its ability to argue its case persuasively.

I: The *Contemporary Significance* of Kaṭha Upaniṣad

The setting for this 'secret teaching' (or '*Upaniṣad*')[2] is an ancient story of a Brahmin's son (called Naciketas) who was unhappy about the sacrificial offerings of his father. The cows being offered were old and feeble; so Naciketas wanted to offer himself. (In case this theme has raised Christian soteriological expectations, I must confess, I do not attempt to draw out any parallel implications from this motif of the son's self-offering). The father became angered by his son's presumption and eventually sent him to his self-chosen doom: 'Unto Yama, god of death, I give you'. The son travelled to Yama's habitat, but had to wait three days, unfed, before Yama returned. To compensate for this deprivation Yama offered the youth any three wishes. Naciketas' third and most important request was for understanding of the meaning of death, and by implication, understanding of the way to immortality.

In the ensuing dialogue, Naciketas makes it clear he was dissatisfied not just with the inadequacy of his father's cows, but with a religious system based on the fulfilment of desire, on the securing of blessings related to this world, even those promising a heavenly world. For, even this entailed constant return to the cycle of life and death. This, then, is the setting for an Upaniṣad that is sufficiently ambiguous in its references to the 'great self', etc., for both theistic and extreme non-dualist interpretation to be possible. Interpretation, therefore, and fidelity to the distinctive kind of vision discovered in and confirmed by the text, is so important for *Viśiṣṭādvaitic* response to a text such as Kaṭha.

The Hermeneutical Process

First then, Kaṭha provides *insight into the hermeneutical process* that is a crucial part of our religious life. Religious people often think of their tradition (their *sanātana dharma*) as having been unchanged from 'the beginning', without reflecting on the continual interaction between text and context, between sacred tradition and other 'worlds' of human experience that impinge on that tradition. The reflection resulting from such interaction *can* prove powerfully creative for the life of the tradition, though no doubt it can also be the opposite of this.

In the Vedāntic tradition of which Kaṭha is part (as part of the *prasthāna-traya*), the process of transmission and therefore of interpretation is said to involve a 3-fold process. Kaṭha I.2.13 is said to refer to this 3-fold process, though slightly different terms are used:

a) There is *śravaṇa*, or 'listening' to the texts, learning the tradition, especially through the guidance of a guru.
b) Then, along with this 'standing-under' the text, there is to be a dynamic process of *manana*, or 'critical reflection' on the meaning of what has been learnt in the texts, and this necessarily involves some degree of re-conceptualising, or re-interpreting (It may well also entail memorising the text). Another way of putting this is to say that the primal symbols and imagery of the traditional text are worked out in concepts meaningful to the seeker, the one compelled by *jijñāsa*, especially the 'desire to know' Brahman. And 'meaning' will always be in relation to context and to historical/cultural conditioning.
c) There is to be *nididhyāsana* or 'contemplation', at which level there is internalised vision, or integral perception of what is ultimately real, the goal of our existence. And in the process of listening, reflecting and visioning, dynamic changes of perception take place.

The seeker is thus always a *pilgrim*, on the move towards the *parama pada*, the 'highest goal', (a term often found in Kaṭha), both in personal attainment and also in interpretation of the tradition from within which the seeking takes place. It is significant that Kaṭha speaks of the seeker as one who (in spite of the need to find an immovable point of peace) is on the move, one who by understanding the driver of the chariot – the 'chariot' being the travelling body - 'reaches the end of the journey' (to use Radhakrishnan's translation of 1.3.9).

This hope of journey's goal reached does not mean that the journeying, the process of seeking to interpret and to understand – and thus the particularities of the seeker's history and culture – are without value and significance (but we return to this point later). However, 'even hearing, many do not know', and it is a 'wondrous' teacher who can impart such skill that the seeker finds this goal that is 'subtlest of the subtle.'[3] Nor 'by reasoning (in itself) is this understanding attainable'; though 'taught by another' (the 'wondrous' teacher perhaps?) the desired understanding can dawn.[4]

This same kind of moving-on hermeneutical process is found even within the text of Kaṭha. Right at the beginning we find Naciketas questioning the efficacy of the ritual practice of his father. A similar pushing out of the meaning-frontiers of inherited myth and ritual is found generally in the Upaniṣads. Kaṭha I.2.11 can be taken as an example of the inner tension between the 'action-section' and the 'insight-section' of the Vedic corpus. There is no question of outright rejection of the tradition, for indeed it is just in the context of the mythic-ritual tradition that the seeking, the questioning, the probing, the reflecting are found in the Upaniṣads. Thus, it is 'as the gifts were taken to the priests' that '*faith* entered him.'[5] And 'faith', far from inducing passive acceptance of whatever was transmitted by way of tradition, prompted a radically *questioning* attitude in Naciketas.

The Upaniṣads are in large part books of *quest* (and therefore questioning) and discovery. In particular they record the search for and insights into the *inner meaning* of Vedic ritual practice. The term 'Upaniṣad' itself has come to mean 'a secret saying', though its literal etymology, 'near-down-sit', again indicates that tradition is the context; for it refers to the respectful approach to what is to be transmitted by teacher to seeker, or from father to son. Perhaps in all our traditions we need this same expectant attitude, the anticipation that there are new insights to be discovered in the sacred text and rituals.

Vaishnavism, after the brilliant hermeneutical synthesis of Rāmānuja and the early Āchāryas, has perhaps not always sufficiently reflected on its tradition with the confident hope of bringing out renewed interpretation through the discovery of fresh insights. Great Vaiṣṇava interpreters of the twentieth century, such as P N Srinivasachari, K C Varadachari, and M Yamunacharya, clearly did have this creative approach, and responding with vision and courage to new philosophical insights, attempted reinterpretation in their various ways. Others now must push further this pioneering hermeneutical frontier as they interact with contemporary life and with other world-views.

The Inter-relating of Religious Traditions

Secondly, closely related to this question of how we interpret our sacred text is the question of *how one religious tradition is to relate to another*. It is often said that *pluralism* is an inescapable feature of contemporary life. In India we might argue that there has been the interaction of many traditions for ages. For example, in using the chariot analogy and then listing the various dimensions of our psycho-physical being, the Upaniṣad clearly refers to and incorporates ideas from the Sāṃkhya system and practice of Yoga associated with it. Yet, in responding to this metaphysical tradition, Kaṭha restates its ideas in a quite *distinctive* way; they are placed within a 'theistic setting' (as even Radhakrishnan notes), just as the Bhagavad Gītā was to do later, repeating some of Kaṭha's verses, and using Buddhist terms as well as Sāṃkhyan.

When religious traditions interact with each other like this, it will necessarily be in a selective, discriminating way, reprocessing ideas and imagery in the light of one's own inner vision, even if that tradition's earlier perceptions also are modified as a result of this interaction. The neo-Vedāntic maxim that 'all religions are in essence the same, all equally valid ways to the same goal', was certainly not what was assumed either in the time of Kaṭha or when Rāmānuja was interpreting it, perhaps sixteen centuries later. It was taken for granted that there will be mutual interaction and appropriation. But this was never indiscriminate, and there was at times also use of violently critical language against the position of others. Today, we rightly eschew such language, and we may well find that engagement with others leads to the discovery of dimensions within our own tradition previously unrecognised; even when the other vision provides a corrective to our own. To condemn all 'cultural appropriation' as necessarily an emasculation of weaker communities by more powerful is surely not an historical reality. However frequently it may also be true, as an all-embracing statement it is, surely, ideological dogmatism?

Kaṭha sees clearly that it is the divine *Mystery*, the continual self-revelation of the divine *beyondness*, that underlies this need for visionary interaction. Kaṭha, for example, affirms – with echoes of a Rigvedic text – 'Wondrous is he who can teach him.....wondrous is he who knows (him).....He is thought of (and spoken of) in many ways. Unless taught by one who knows him as himself, there is no going thither, for he is inconceivable, subtler than the subtle.'[6]

However convinced we may be of the truth of our own vision, no one system will totally exhaust the meaning of that Being whose mystery we all seek to understand. We have so much to learn from each other, so much to contribute to each other, if we are to be faithful to 'He who is,'[7] the Beyond, the One who is 'thought of in many ways'.

If, however, there is to be the interaction of genuine dialogue, the distinctive features of the world-view in which we are grounded need to be brought out forcefully. Mutuality of learning is essential, but the *difference* between the ontology – and therefore the theology, epistemology and even the ethical stance – of, for example, Viśiṣṭa-advaita and Kevala-advaita should not be lost. The distinctive stance of each has to be brought out in the interpretation of a text such as Kaṭha. Those whose *darśana*, whose vision of reality, emphasises that the distinctions within the continuum of being are of the essence of that being's nature, should not weakly concede that this is merely an inferior understanding of the trans-relational nature of reality.

In Kaṭha, for example, there is reference to that 'primal God, difficult-to-be-seen, deeply hidden,'[8] 'the Self, smaller than the small, greater than the great, set in the heart of every creature,'[9] 'the Self who is attained only by the one chosen by that self.... the one to whom the self reveals his own nature,'[10] 'the supreme abode of the All-pervading,'[11] 'the Person beyond the unmanifest', where there is 'the end of the journey, the final goal.'[12] There is every reason for Viśiṣṭādvaitins to continue to identify this as that supremely personal Being who is – to use a favourite phrase of Rāmānuja – 'the abode of countless glorious attributes', 'the supreme Object of loving worship'; in other words the eternally 'Distinguished One'. In the dialogical encounter of religions this distinctive theistic vision is crucial.

The Role of Symbolic Imagery

Thirdly, there is throughout Kaṭha a rich use of *symbolic imagery* that would *counter any literalist interpretation of the tradition*, or indeed a purely rationalistic view of what is the truth of things. We can point out just a few of these symbols and a little of the symbolic imagery, that provide windows into our view of reality. At the outset there is the portrayal of Death in the mythic imagery of Yama, who in turn becomes the teacher disclosing the larger truth of existence that Naciketas desired to know. Then Agni (Fire), as mediator of the sacrifice, is seen as 'the aid to heaven....the means for attaining the boundless world, the support (of the universe), yet abiding in the secret place (of the heart).'[13] Through meditation on Agni (and knowing the inner meaning of the fire-sacrifice) the wise person 'throws off the bonds of death, overcomes sorrow, rejoices in the world of heaven.'[14] Then in II.1.12-13 the inner self is said to be like a flame without any obscuring smoke. Agni here clearly carries potent symbolic meaning for the whole process of moving from the earth-bound to a higher level of wisdom and being.

Then there are images of plant-life ('a mortal ripens like corn, and like corn is born again' (I.1.6); there is the cosmic tree (to which we return later); and there is the bridge to be crossed[15] – because of which we need to 'arise and be awake....for sharp as the edge of a razor and hard to cross is that path' (an image found in a number of other Upaniṣads, as well as in Zoroastrian and Islamic traditions). Then, inner psychic life is likened to a chariot going on its journey, drawn by horses, controlled by reins in the hand of the lord of the chariot,[16] and is also likened to a city with eleven gates.[17] There is also an image of the inner Self 'as the sun, not tainted by the faults of the eye.'[18] Or there is the 'eternal Lord, the size of the thumb, dwelling in the midst of the body....

like a flame without smoke.'[19] And perhaps most impressive of all, the image of light: 'Everything shines only after that shining light. His shining illumines all this world.'[20] Again, this a common image in the Upaniṣads (and the Gītā) as well as in other religious traditions.

The above is more than sufficient to indicate the range of imagery in Kaṭha, whether used as seemingly simple metaphor, or intended to carry more primal depth of religious consciousness. The question is, however, what does this mean for the way in which truth is revealed to us through our tradition and its language?

Religions as 'Symbol-Systems'?

It has become fashionable to describe religious traditions as 'symbol-systems'. In itself such a term is non-judgmental. If we mean, though, that nothing in our scriptures or traditions has more than metaphoric value, and therefore little if any *direct correspondence* to reality, Vaiṣṇavas and others who view their religious experience with ontic and epistemic *realism*, will surely protest.

If nothing objective in our religious experience bears *direct* correspondence to the ultimately real, we are looking at reality and at divine transcendence in a thoroughly *advaitic* manner (Advaita in some ways being an ancient form of post-modernism!), very close to Śaṅkara's *lakṣaṇārtha* view of scripture, its language and its imagery. Rāmānuja's epistemic realism, as with many other thorough-going theists – Hindu and Christian – argued rather that theological statements do correspond to reality, in a direct sense, even though no such descriptions are in any way *exhaustive* of the divine mystery. The 'otherness' of God (*paratva*) is as essential as the 'nearness' or 'accessibility' (*saulabhya*) of God, as Vaiṣṇava theology has consistently affirmed.

Rāmānuja's Relational Epistemology

The Upaniṣadic '*Neti, neti*' for Rāmānuja meant that none of our descriptions of God are exhaustive: 'Not thus only' is what must be acknowledged. Maybe there is a fine epistemological line to be drawn here between the extremes of objectivist literalism and subjectivist illusionism (or absolute relativism!). In Viśiṣṭādvaitic thought this dilemma is resolved by a thoroughly *relational* epistemology: both subject and object are real and in their real interaction mediate truth and meaning. Revelation is a relational process.

Thus, in Viśiṣṭādvaita we find the centrality of *analogy* in the revelatory process, especially the self-body controlling analogy. Thus, too, the paradox of Kaṭha: 'Not through transient things is that abiding One reached; yet....by impermanent means have I reached the everlasting.'[21] The Mystery *is* mediated to us within our embodied being, especially by means of the divine embodiedness alongside our being. Such revelatory embodiedness is quite central to Viśiṣṭādvaitic theology, though there is, in the final analysis, equal emphasis upon the *immediacy* of divine revelation. 'Mediated immediacy' – a phrase used by a Christian theologian [22] to describe 'Our Knowledge of God', is at the heart of the Viśiṣṭādvaitic vision, and is of a piece with a tradition in which imagery is central.

God 'not reachable by argument'

It is of a piece, too, with a tradition which took very seriously Kaṭha's contention that the divine Mystery is, in the end, *atarkyam* – 'unreachable by argument', 'unknowable by logical means of proof'. It is good to find trends within modern epistemology countering earlier positivist constraints of strict empiricism on the one hand and inferential logic on the other. We should not, of course, lay the blame for all this on western modernity, with its secularising trends. A strictly empiricist approach to life, valuing only what is 'known' on the evidence of the senses and rational inference thereon, affirming an essentially hedonist ethic, were precisely the principles expounded by the ancient Indian school of Lokāyata! And which western philosophy has given more emphasis to rational logic than did the powerful Indian school of Nyāya?

As we have seen in several other chapters in this book, all the Vedāntins were agreed that knowledge of *Brahman,* the supreme Self of all, cannot be dependent upon such inferential forms of thinking, even if some Vedāntins, Śaṅkara in particular, often make effective use of inference to find clues to the existence and character of *Brahman*. Significantly, it was only Rāmānuja who gave an extensive critique of Nyāya's claim to know God through inference rather than by means of divine revelation. Clearly, he felt that if God can be inferentially proven, he becomes an object among other objects. Indeed, the God of Nyāya looks rather like a *primus inter pares*, or the first among equals, rather than the Ground and Goal of all being.

Recognising the Mystery

Kaṭha recognises clearly the *mystery* of the supreme Self, to know whom merely objective knowledge would be quite incommensurate. But neither is the knowledge of this Self wholly subjective. Reference has already been made to the way Kaṭha finds the supreme Self's ambivalent presence in the universe: 'That primal God, difficult to be seen, deeply hidden, set in the cave of the heart, dwelling in the deep....' Then it is affirmed that such a God can be realised – through *ādhyātma-yoga*, the practice of deeply spiritual engagement.[23] Or again: we are to know the Self as 'the bodiless among bodies, the stable among the unstable, the great, the all-pervading....'[24]. And again: 'The Self, though hidden in all beings, does not shine forth (openly) but can be seen by subtle seers through their sharp and subtle insight.'[25]

There is here a clear awareness of the danger of a merely objectifying approach to the Ultimate: 'The Self is not to be sought through the senses....' Some, though, merely 'look outward and not within', not beyond their objective existence to the inner meaning, the inner mystery of things. What is to be realised is that God is 'the one inner Controller, the inmost Self of all'[26] – titles especially beloved by Rāmānuja. And for the wise who can thus perceive him within the whole life of the universe, 'there is eternal peace'.

Towards the end of the twentieth century it was recognised by an increasing number of philosophers of science, as well as in the behavioural sciences such as sociology, that even in our most 'objective' knowing, we cannot, and perhaps should not, attempt to escape completely our human subjectivity. And even in the natural sciences, where absolute objectivity has been assumed to be the ideal, many now recognise that there are hidden, intuitionally formed dimensions in the scientific process, what Polanyi called the 'tacit dimension.'[27] Thus, all true knowledge seems to involve a subject/object dialectic – again, central to Rāmānuja's epistemology – and it is a fallacy to assume that the only valid knowledge is that which is 'objectively' proven. Perhaps there is literally no-thing that should be taken only as empirically observable. And this will call, in the final analysis, for an immediacy of perception.

The Supreme Being's Initiative Needed

Fourthly, a point that may seem at first to be very different from the above, whereas we find eventually that they interlink. For, I now move on to Kaṭha's clear affirmation of the *initiative and sovereignty of the supreme Self in the process of understanding divine truth.* Radical theists tend to speak of 'divine grace' when referring to our dependence upon the divine initiative or to our need for God's self-revealing. The passage referred to here is not quite so explicit: 'This Self....is to be attained only by the one whom (the Self) chooses. To such a one the Self reveals his own nature.'[28] Earlier I referred to the Vedantic discipline of hearing, reflecting and visioning required of the seeker. Kaṭha, however, denies categorically that any such *sādhana* is sufficient *in itself* to discover the inner reality of things. All we seekers can do, really, is to confess that 'He is': 'When he is apprehended as existent, his real nature becomes clear.'[29] If we are to probe this Mystery, then, it must be because *the Mystery itself seeks to manifest itself to us*; it must be an innate characteristic of the Mystery that is self-revealing.

This is not merely a theological truth. Despite the wonderful range of knowledge that has been acquired through modern scientific endeavour, despite all the ingenuity of modern technology, despite the impressive mastery of the empirical world that has been achieved, in the end we can know only as much of the universe as the universe is ready to reveal of herself to us.

And though what has been 'revealed' is immense and wonderful, it only serves to emphasise just how much more immense is the unknown world lying beyond, yet to be understood. The more we know, the more we know we do not know.

Confronted both by the vastness of the universe, by the mystery of our every experience of this universe, and then by the great Mystery beyond this universe, we need above all *humility*. What anyone who would seek to penetrate the underlying Reality of things needs above all is modesty, meekness, awe, reverence, trust. There is no place here for the hubris, the overweening pride in human achievement that has characterised far too much modern technology.

Or, we might think of this needed attitude by reference to the revered Vaiṣṇava term, *bhakti*. For, *bhakti* seems to be the only fitting response to this mysterious universal Self who discloses his inner being to us by his gracious choice so to do. As well as reverence, *bhakti* includes the devotion of love and trust, a participant relationship.

Kaṭha does not bring out explicitly the full personal dimensions usually characterising a Being who 'chooses' and who is self-disclosing. There is, of course, the diversely interpreted *dhātuh-prasādāt* in 1.2.20, which can mean, either 'grace of the creator', or 'tranquillity of the senses' (very different though these two may seem). When the same phrase occurs in Śvetāvatara Upaniṣad the former meaning is clear: here we have to admit that there is room for uncertainty.

Even so, in the end, it is the sense of humble, loving, participant relationship that will surely most fully express knowledge of, reflection on and understanding of the universal Mystery. To use the language of Viśiṣṭādvaita, in the end *jñāna* (knowledge, inner realisation) is to be seen as *bhakti*, and the culminating point of *bhakti* is that self-giving surrender, or *prapatti*, that is the only appropriate response to the self-giving and self-revealing of the supreme Self. Reference to '*prapatti*' does, of course, raise possibly divisive questions for Śrī-Vaiṣṇavas, given their once tragic conflict between the Ten-galai and Vadagalai sects, in particular on the role of '*prapatti*' in the process of liberation. That debate was far from meaningless: in view of the divine 'beyondness', in some way only a divine initiative will suffice to help seeking souls cross the bridge, that difficult and razor-fine link between the world and the *parama padam*, who is at the same time the 'all-pervading One'.

Ecological Implications

Finally, a particular ethical issue, wide-ranging in its ramifications, probably the greatest crisis of our times: *human pollution and destruction of the earth*, in brief, the environmental or *ecological crisis*. And, as a counter to this growing threat to earth's life, Kaṭha does provide us with some clear clues. Obviously, there is no explicit cognisance of the modern forms of this problem. The roots of the crisis are diverse; but we cannot ignore the tendency in modern life to technological arrogance, an aggressiveness that seeks to master and destructively exploit the natural world and its resources. Nature, the earth and the other primal elements are seen as having value only from the standpoint of their usefulness to humans.

Thus, there is a dichotomy seen between human life and the natural world. This dualism of western thought (especially since Descartes, whose ontological criterion was 'I think, and therefore I am') is one of rational mind versus irrational nature, with the belief that mind so transcends nature as to be able, by innate right, to master and exploit nature to further human interests.

The first requirement for countering this dangerously anthropocentric attitude towards the world is a new vision of human life and the *life of nature as inter-dependent and inter-penetrating*. The human race certainly has very special powers over nature and special responsibilities therefore to care for nature. But humanity must not forget that it is the earth that sustains human existence; without her abundant sustenance the human race perishes.

In what ways does Kaṭha help to evoke a vision of human participation in nature? Such 'dualism' as there is in the Upaniṣad, and in Indian thought as a whole if we crudely generalise, is that of transcendent, immutable *self* (and selfhood too has its microcosmic and its macrocosmic dimensions) and mutable, active *nature*. Human life, as all creaturely life, is comprised of and shares in both these two cosmic entities. While mainstream Indian thought in a number of its forms of expression sees tension between self and nature, or soul and nature, never does it believe there is *need for the one to master and exploit the other*. Indeed, the goal of life usually is quite the opposite. Far more often the aim is to achieve the *detachment* of one from the other through the control of mind and senses.

The Upaniṣad's Pointers to Cosmic Sensitivity

It is in Kaṭha's second part especially that we find a number of points pertinent to this issue. I would point to four primal images of the cosmos and its life that carry far-reaching implications for ecological sensitivity:

a) I take the last of these images first: in 2.3.1 we have striking reference to the *Cosmic Tree*, an image that is also to be found in other primal religious traditions. It normally stands for the centre point of cosmic life and the world of nature, the *axis mundi*. Now we have to admit that this cosmic tree image is viewed very differently in different contexts, as can be seen by a comparison of Ṛgveda 1.24.7, Chāndogya 6.11, Maitrī 6.4, Śvetāsvatara 3.9, Samyutta Nikaya 4.160, Bhagavad Gītā 15.1-4. In general, the Buddhist text and the Gītā see the tree as symbol of that sap of life – passion, hatred, delusion – which is to be destroyed root and branch. The Gītā goes on, though, to affirm the need to seek refuge in the Source of this cosmic tree of life.

In the Ṛgveda and Upaniṣads generally the tree of life is interpreted more positively. Here in Kaṭha this cosmic fig-tree, with its strange upside-down look – roots upwards, branches downwards – stands for Brahman as that central and steadfast Reality in which 'all the worlds rest', or 'are established.'[30] Thus, it refers to Brahman in manifest, cosmic life-giving form. There is no tension here between Brahman as Ground of all beings, and the tree as Brahman manifest in thrusting, thriving cosmic life. The text goes on: 'The whole world, whatever here exists, springs from and moves in life.'[31] And this is said to induce awe, even fearful trembling, such is the mystery of the throbbing life of the universe and its creatures. This attitude towards nature's life is clearly opposed to either the aggressive destruction of earth and her resources, or an indifferent neglect of nature.

b) Then, earlier, there is a different kind of image. It is said that 'looking inward', i.e. into the inner reality lying beyond empirical life, 'the wise man sees the Self....the experiencer (the honey-eater), the *living Spirit close at hand*, as Lord of past and future.'[32] Then this inmost Self is identified with three deities, including *Aditi*, the boundless Mother, Mother-nature, the soul of the gods. Thus, the inner Self (and in this instance we may assume that both individual self and universal Self are indicated) has this close affinity with the whole boundless world of nature, a perception with immediate implications for how humans are to relate to and act towards nature.

c) Then comes the affirmation of the *togetherness*, the *one-ness of all beings*. 'Who sees many-ness goes to death.'[33] An ontological continuity is claimed for all life. If, however, we go on to interpret this one-ness in a way that makes inevitable a complementing doctrine of *cosmic illusion*, with all the multiform distinctiveness of the world quite unreal from the ultimate perspective of the one-ness, as dominant forms of Advaita do, then I believe we are on a path that is equally threatening to nature's life, the threat of ultimate indifference. Such an interpretation of nature (and of *māyā*) surely undermines any commitment to an earth-caring life. It is not this kind of 'togetherness', 'non-manyness' that is envisaged by Kaṭha, and has been vigorously denied by Viśiṣṭādvaita.

d) Finally, we find repeated reference to the 'inner Self of all' (*sarva-bhūtāntara-ātmā*) who is the '*one Controller*'. Along with this there are 'the wise who perceive him as abiding within (all), (for whom) there is eternal peace.'[34] The obvious corollary to such an all-pervading inner Self is to see the *whole cosmos as his body* – integrated, invigorated, controlled, made ultimately real by this indwelling Self of all. And this is Viśiṣṭādvaita's key doctrine, brought out so explicitly and prominently by Rāmānuja (as explained in the second chapter above). To see that as the secret of our cosmic life and our relationship with earth, says Kaṭha, is to move towards a life of peace – peace with each other, peace with nature, peace with all her creatures, the 'eternal peace' grounded in the peace of the supreme Self of all.

As one grounded in Christian theological tradition, I find so much in Kaṭha that resonates with my own vision of things, and much too that helps me re-vision that Christian tradition. It is only from a Christian-Viśiṣṭādvaita perspective that I find this 'resonating' interpretation of Kaṭha. Vaiṣṇavas need to affirm more clearly the distinctive stance – ontologically, epistemologically, theologically – of their Viśiṣṭādvaitic tradition. And I am deeply convinced that we need more of such interactive and dialogical reflection on our contemporary human situation.

Endnotes

1. Papers from the first two seminars were published in *Studies in Rāmānuja*, Madras: Rāmānuja Vedānta Centre 1980: and *Śrī Andal: Her Contribution to Literature, Philosophy, Religion and Art*, Madras: Rāmānuja Vedānta Centre, 1986.
2. See e.g. *The Principal Upaniṣads*, (Edited with Introduction, Text Translation Notes) by S. Radhakrishnan, London: Allen and Unwin, 1953.
3. I.2.7-8
4. I.2.9
5. I.1.2
6. I.2.7-8
7. II.3.12
8. I.2.12
9. I.2.20
10. I.2.23
11. I.3.9
12. I.3.10
13. I.1.14
14. I.1.18
15. I.3.2
16. I.3.3
17. II.2.1
18. II.2.11
19. II.1.12-13
20. II.2.15

21. I.2.10
22. John Baillie in *Our Knowledge of God*, London: OUP 1939.
23. I.2.12
24. I.2.22
25. I.3.12
26. II.2.12
27. M. Polanyi, *Personal Knowledge*, London: Routledge 1958; Cf. also his *Science, Faith and Society*, Oxford 1946, and *Knowing and Being*, London: Routledge, 1969.
28. I.2.23
29. II.3.12-13
30. II.3.1
31. II.3.2
32. II.1.5
33. II.1.10-11
34. II.2.22

S

7

The Epiphanic Body: How Images and Concepts Relate

Religious life in all its dimensions is deeply and dependently interlocked with symbolic imagery. Our belief systems, our religious communities, our ways of praying and expressing our religiousness, even those special ethical convictions we have about living in the right way – all lose their life-springs, their creative matrix, if our distinctive imagery is lost. Not that image-breakers, or iconoclasts, have no place in ecclesial life. For it is in the innate nature of all institutions, Hindu and Christian, to sacralise and mythologise images whose power must be broken if our community life is to be free from 'idolatry', if the divine Spirit is to find true and free expression in and through our life in God's world. Human existence is never free from ambiguity.

Immediately, then, we see something of the dialectic involved. To put this in Christian terms, those images by which the church lives are necessarily born out of our human engagement with the world. All our sacred images, in all religious life, emerge from earth-related images – of birth, growth, journeying, suffering, dying; elemental images from earth's seasons and fecundity; cultural images from the social milieu with which religions interact; even those special images from our distinctive ecclesial tradition, with the Jesus-story at the centre. Thus, memory and the impact of crucial moments of our history, lie deep in our community consciousness. All our most potent imagery derives from the interface of the Spirit's engagement with the life of the world; it encapsulates epiphanic moments in that engagement.

Why is it, then, that there has been so little theological reflection in India on the role of imagery? Or, to put this a little differently, what is the innate connection between images and conceptual systems? How do theologies relate to the symbols undergirding them?[1]

In this chapter, I propose to subject just one faith-image, that of the *body*, to an analysis seeking to discover what role the 'body' has in religious reflection, how such imagery is 'embodied' in our conceptualising of reality. This will be a cross-cultural, comparative analysis. For, as with a number of other images, *the body is crucial to many faith-systems* other than Christian. And, more than others perhaps, missiologists, living and reflecting on the boundaries between Christian faith and other worlds of faith and culture, should be aware of and be able to engage with those other faiths and cultures. It is unfortunate that attitudes in India today – socially, religiously, culturally, politically – have become so divisive that 'engagement' of the kind explored in these essays has become a cause for suspicion and resentment.

The Body as 'Epiphanic' in India's Faiths

Firstly, what are some of the ways in which the body is taken as in some sense *epiphanic* in religious traditions? Here we shall, necessarily, be brief and selective:

(a) Climb the hill at Shravana Belagola in Karnataka, or explore the caves of Ajanta, and it becomes immediately obvious that the colossal iconic *body* of a Jaina Tīrthānkara (a 'ford-crosser') or of a Buddha is experienced as *epiphanic* in the meditative life of Jains and Buddhists. In fact, it is quite possible that the post-Vedic introduction of image-*pūjā* in Brāhmāṇic Hinduism was the direct result of the Buddha's popular role throughout much of India as object of veneration and aid to meditation. Even for the

Jaina tradition - that in its more extreme forms has been body-mortifying - cosmologically the universe is seen as body-shaped (as also in primal Vedic perceptions of the cosmos).[2]

And in the more inclusive Mahāyāna ('Great Vehicle') Buddhism it is explicitly the Buddha's three-fold body (*tri-kāya*) that, at three different levels of existence, is seen as epiphanic. There is the *dharma-kāya*, the transcendent essence of Buddha-ness; there is the *sambhoga-kāya* (literally, 'body of enjoyment'), referring to the radiant celestial body; there is the *nirmāṇa-kāya*, the body of 'transformation' when the Buddha appears on earth in human form.

(b) Within the multiple forms of the Hindu traditions we might note just three:

(i) In the Hero-Saivism of the (often anti-Brāhmaṇic) Lingāyata tradition of Karnataka, the Linga at the centre of cult and thought is depicted in a three-fold way reminiscent of the Buddha's *tri-kāya* forms. The Linga is taken as the embodiment of Śiva in the three forms of *Iṣṭa, Prāṇa*, and *Bhāva*, being differing levels of apprehension by corresponding forms of the *Aṅga* or soul (literally, a 'limb'). The three forms of Śiva's 'body' also correspond to the three innate forms of every body-material, subtle and causal. This highly moralistic reform movement in Karnataka for which Basava in the 12th century was pivotal, ruled out altogether the Linga's sexual connotations as found in various Purāṇic sources.

(ii) Just prior to Basava there was the immensely significant advent of Śrī-Vaiṣṇava's great Āchārya, Rāmānuja. Though teaching in the 11th century, Rāmānuja drew on rich and diverse streams of tradition in formulating his *deha-dehī-bhāva* (also known as *śarīra-śarīrī-bhāva*), or body-self-signification/realisation.[3] He was able to point to key texts in the Vedic/Upanishadic corpus, especially the Bṛhadāraṇyaka passage that repeatedly refers to 'He who dwells in the earth (etc) .. whose body the earth is, who controls the earth from within, he is your self, the inner controller, the immortal' (III.7). Rāmānuja also drew on images at the heart of the Bhagavad Gītā, especially the *viśva-rūpa-darśana* section (chap.11, the 'vision' of Krishna in 'the form of the universe') which explicitly identifies the whole of cosmic life with the body of God. Less overt is his indebtedness to the *bhakti*-songs of the Āḻvārs several centuries earlier than Rāmānuja, who repeatedly express their burning desire for '*darśana* of the body of God', and extol the beauties and glories of that divine body.

The Potent Contribution of Rāmānuja

Probably *avatāra*-faith itself made another potent contribution to Rāmānuja's body-centred theology (see esp. chapters 3 and 5 above). In part this can be said simply because the Avatar-figure, especially (though not exclusively) Kṛṣṇa in the case of the Śrī-Vaiṣṇavas, is the focal-point of *bhakti*-experience, and that experience in turn becomes central to cosmological perception. Along with this, though, Rāmānuja's metaphysical *realism* must be taken note of.[4] Rāmānuja categorically and explicitly argued that avataric bodies were *real,* in the same way as the creative process is real because it shares in the life of the divine body. As God is real, cosmic life is real; as cosmic life is real, the avatāra body is real. Thus, for Rāmānuja, soteriology and cosmology are of a piece. As we saw earlier, this was not so with Śaṅkara, that creative process itself cannot be *real* in the sense that the supreme Self is real.

In Rāmānuja's case, however, we could equally begin at the other end and suggest that the cosmos is, for him, the *real body* of God because the embodiment in the *avatāra* is the focal point of religious vision and thus informs all cosmic perception. In analysing Vaiṣṇava spirituality, though, we noted the strong link between the *avatāra* and the *arcā,* or the sacred image so important to the cultic, especially Pāñcarātra tradition that fed into Vaiṣṇavism. Indeed, images themselves are often described as avataric. This strong iconic tradition was crucial in the development of their *deha-dehī* theology (i.e. that the whole world is an 'inseparably related' body for God, its inner transcending Self). Yet, he is never *explicit* about the role of sacred images, other than what he writes about the Vedāntic practice of symbol-meditation.

Later Śrī-Vaiṣṇava Theology

Later Śrī-Vaiṣṇava theologians, especially the Ten-galais or the 'southern' sect that taught the cat-way of divine grace, are very clear that sacral images are revelatory of 'the greatest grace of the Lord, that being free he becomes bound, being independent he becomes dependent on his devotees for all the service he receives... Yes, the Infinite becomes finite, that the child-like soul may grasp, understand and love him.'[5]

It is significant too, that Śrī-Vaiṣṇava temples, or *Divya-deśas*, are also seen as shaped in the form of the body.

To sum up the above: Vaiṣṇava theology of the earth, indeed of the whole universe, which describes it as the 'body of God', draws on richly diverse streams of Hindu tradition, and arrives at a vision of God as wonderfully beyond creation, yet mysteriously within it, controlling and loving a creation with which God's essential selfhood is 'inseparably connected', yet remains eternally free, fulfilled, constant – the 'embodiment of countless glorious qualities'.

Equally diverse, of course, were the streams feeding into *Śaiva* religious life. And the systematic Śaiva theology that emerged not long after Rāmānuja also described the world as the 'body' of God. This perception, however, never became pivotal as in Śrī-Vaiṣṇava teaching.

The Significance of the Yoga Tradition

(iii) Another important stream flowing into each of the complex traditions mentioned above – Buddhism, the Gītā, Advaita, Viśiṣṭādvaita, Śaiva religion – is that of *Yoga,* though it was variously appropriated within each, and therefore had different 'meaning' within each. The key to the many-hued world of Yoga is its perception of the body as a micro-cosmic version of the macro-cosmos. (There is a similar micro-macro correspondence found between the sacrifice and the world in Vedic ritual life). Yoga, then, especially Tantric Yoga, envisions an inner structure, with psychic power-points channelled throughout the body, enabling inner latent potencies to develop and the self to reach its true destiny, either in its *kaivalya* state of 'splendid isolation' free from all relativity, or in union with the supreme Self located subtly within the individual self.

In this liberating process, however, there is usually in Yoga a tensive dialectic between soul and body, or between Puruṣa and Prakṛti to use the categories of the Sāṃkhya metaphysics so often linked with Yoga's liberative techniques or *sādhanas,* especially in the Gīta. The imagery Sāṃkhya often used for the realm of nature to which the body belongs was that of a seducing dancer, unveiling herself in the presence of the bewitched soul. Nature is also said to be like a blind person, lacking awareness and dependent upon, yet providing movement for, that 'lame' or immobile being, the soul. Only by these two contrasting strands coming close to each other, however, is the creative process set in motion.

In Tantrik practice, often linked with Yoga, and equally pervasive in Indian religious traditions, the body is significant in several ways, some explicitly sexual. We here note only the central place of the *maṇḍala*, the diagrammatic circle (occasionally square) which Tantra also takes as imaging both the body and the cosmos. Meditation on the *maṇḍala*, therefore, may well involve the touching of corresponding parts of the body and relating this to corresponding elemental or cosmic powers. The body is crucial for whatever liberative goal is envisaged.

An Underlying Primal Influence

(c) There is good reason to believe that underlying all the above Indian perceptions of the body is a prior *primal* worldview in which the body is central, especially as expressed in sacred dance, mythic story and epiphanic experience. This is of special importance in understanding too the cultural roots of a *Dalit* worldview. Four features essential to the primal vision stand out in this context:

(i) The sense of belonging to and sharing intimately in *earth's life*, of deriving from and being nurtured by Earth, perhaps perceived as a great Mother, in any case seen as possessing vital powers upon which all earthlings depend. In *Totemic* cultural/ religious tradition, particular life-forms (animals, birds, trees, etc) are taken as being focal points of sacred power – another cultural expression of this earth-groundedness. We can note that many clan-names among Telugu 'Dalit' communities (the name of a tree, hill, animal, bird, or some other life-form in the natural world) reflect this 'totemic' cultural tradition. Even where no clear expression of Totemism appears, there is invariably the expectation that sacral power can impinge upon human life, often unexpectedly, at many different places of epiphany, especially trees, streams, hills, rocks, earth and specific birds and animals.

(ii) The sense of belonging to and sharing in a cohesive *community body*, with festival occasions – characterized by dance, song and ritual – enhances such a sense of corporate identity. Initiation into the community (usually for males) is often through acts of deprivation and heroism, with life-long taboos (often involving bodily functions) strengthening community bonding. Community life is experienced as an extension of bodily life.

(iii) The sense of shared life-enhancement by means of *shared sacred acts and power-channelling devices:* from common marking or adorning of the body or the house with signs of the sacred, to festive drum and annual sacrifice (perhaps of the sacred totem with feasting on its flesh). Similar means are used also to avert the danger of harmful powers.

(iv) There is the expectation that gifted members of the community body will function as 'charismatic' leaders: creative story-tellers and singers (even if based closely on given tradition), drummers, dreamers, diviners, demon-exorcisers, healers – with women exercising such gifts in many communities. References to Yoga, sacrifice, focal points of sacrality, micro-macro-cosmic structures, etc., should not, therefore, be dismissed merely as manifestations of classical elitism, and hence of oppressive hierarchical traditions, however effectively they may have become 'co-opted' by special classes dominating community life.

With the above as the four most invariable marks of 'primal' life, we can properly conclude that deeply embedded within the body-related imagery of the so-called 'great traditions' lie strands of this primal cultural life.

Body-Images within Christian Tradition

(d) We have still to note the place of body-imagery within Christian traditions. Three pointers will suffice:

(i) While the biblical witness does not refer to cosmic life as God's 'body', but usually as that which is 'wonderfully made', 'put in place', etc., as though by a Great Carpenter or Composer, there are certainly many references to God's 'eye', 'hand', 'foot', 'heart', etc, describing God at work within human and natural history. God transcendent, in other words, is often expressed in terms of God immanent, and as though relating to the human and natural worlds through a body. Both Jewish and Christian traditions, of course, deny that God literally has a body, as this would compromise God's transcendent perfection. Perhaps this is the reason for the prohibition of 'graven images'. Some scholars, however, see lying behind this, a taboo on the depiction of God's sexuality.[6] There must be no body for God because then, as in the religion of the 'pagans', it becomes necessary to depict sexual parts. Perhaps in our cultural histories – Indian and European – there is a link here.

Three crucial topics in the New Testament, however, put body imagery right at the centre. There is the explicit reference to the body of Jesus as instrument of divine blessing (peace, salvation) to the world; and that body is described as a divine 'embodiment.'[7] Then, there is the great emphasis in the gospel stories on the healing or 'wholeness' of bodies, or their 'salvation', including 'peace' to the body of nature – again through the presence and healing power of Jesus. We still need more reflection on the nature and meaning of that healing ministry, pointing as it does to the overcoming of evil, the breaking in of God's reign, and the hope of the body of glory in eternity.[7a]

Thirdly, there is the strong Pauline image of the Jesus-community as the 'body of Christ.'[8] The intention of this image is both to point to the unity and togetherness of all 'members', under the one Head, in spite of the many distinctive roles within this one body, and to point to the importance of diversity and of the distinctive functions of various 'members', prompted by the one Spirit, for building up the life of the whole body. Paul does not explicitly extend this image to include all humanity, or all creation, though in places this would seem to be implied. For example:

> He is the image of the unseen God...
> All things were created through him and for him...
> And in him all things hold together,
> and he is the Head of the Body, that is, the Church...
> God wanted all fullness to be found in him....
> everything in heaven and everything on earth.[9]

The Eucharistic 'Body'

(ii) The sacramental tradition of the church, based on the gospel witness to eucharistic bread as 'the body of Christ', is another key body-image, potent in the liturgical and devotional life of the Christian community, and sometimes linked with such extra-biblical imagery as that of 'the sacred heart' of Jesus. Here, too, we should note the linkage of this eucharistic imagery with that of rites of initiation in which the body is washed, anointed and marked with the sign of the cross, and thus initiated into the community 'body' of Christ – in the rite of Confirmation this being seen as the body that shares in the ministry of the Anointed One.[10]

A More Inclusive Body-Theology

iii) Recent Christian emphasis has been, on the one hand – in the liturgical movement and through Vatican II generally – on the recovery of this sense of the *whole* body being the worshipping, serving 'body of Christ'. Further, the ecumenical spirit has been even more inclusive – in eco-theology,[11] process[12] and evolutionary theology, such as that of Teilhard de Chardin,[13] in many expressions of indigenous theology, in creation spirituality,[14] and especially eco-feminist theology.[15] All these, even if indirectly, relate to that 'primal' sense of the whole creation as the Body of God (developed most systematically by the Hindu theologian, Rāmānuja, as we noted above), with that creation-body providing the grounding life which humans also share. The notion of a sustaining, motherly earth-body is, of course, also at the centre of the world-view of many for whom theistic belief is anathema: to certain kinds of 'new age' and eco-feminist thinkers for example.

Indian-Christian Theology

Although a few theologians in India have explored themes of embodiment,[16] and a few have seen a 'preparation for the gospel' in such a body-theology as that of Rāmānuja, most have assumed (a) if classical tradition is favoured, as with earlier Catholic scholars, and a few non-Catholics such as Stanley Samartha and K. P. Aleaz, that it is the Advaitic tradition that provides the most appropriable metaphysical framework for authentic Indian Christian theologising; or (b) that a Latin American style of Liberation Theology, assuming radical discontinuity with any classically expressed cultural tradition, provides our most compulsive pointers. Until the 1990s, many Indian theologians influenced by liberationist thought, including Dalit writers,[17] have regarded eco-theology as yet another attempt by affluent westerners to seduce the third world from its primary task of affirming and fighting for justice for oppressed people. At last it begins to appear that Indian theologians recognise that there can be no *economy*-based justice without a radical change in *ecological* attitudes. True eco-justice, or *oikos*-justice, involves both human bodies and the body of God's earth.[18]

Human Ambiguity about the Body

At this point we must note again the fact of human ambiguity – in this case specifically the ambiguous nature of human embodiment. Every one of the religious traditions whose body-talk has been referred to above has, albeit in distinctive ways, been aware of this ambiguity. On the other hand, much creation spirituality seems oblivious of this ambiguous character of human existence. Eco-feminism is certainly aware of flawed human embodiedness, but tends to identify this with male perversions of body-perception and body-experience, thus reversing the tendency in many male-dominated traditions to locate the moral ambivalence, even the problem, in the female body.

It is the body as such, though, that is ambivalent in most traditions. The contradiction of 'flesh' and 'spirit' that the Apostle identifies[19] at the centre of the human dilemma is not, of course, a simple body-soul dichotomy. 'Flesh' is that fallen part of our human nature that is in opposition to the renewing work of God's Spirit within us. Yet the anguished cry, 'Who will set me free from this body of death?,'[20] does indicate also something of the ambivalence Paul feels about his own, and every unrenewed body.[21] As we shall note later in this essay, the Apostle also uses the body-image in very positive ways.

In spite of frequent claims to the contrary, there is also considerable ambiguity in almost all Indian religious traditions, with the exception of the hedonistic materialists, the Lokayatas, who disappeared as a belief-system quite early. Yoga, for example, in its diverse forms is essentially concerned with 'yoking' the mind in its tendency to be misled by sensory experience and thus by attachment to the objects of the senses found in the natural world. In classical Yoga the goal is to set free the self truly to be it-self, not in relation to the objective world, but as transcendent to it in 'splendid isolation' (*kaivalya*).

Similar ambiguity is found in Buddhist traditions in varying degrees. The body, and the female body especially in classical accounts of the Buddha's tradition, is prone to delude the one seeking the ultimate state of peace and bliss. Jainism, with its rigorous ascetic practice of body-mortification as the way of soul-purification, is even more explicit on the issue. There is a basic ontological as well as a soteriological dichotomy of the two categories, matter and soul. Similarly, for Śaṅkara's Advaita, only the way of *sannyāsa*, the renouncing of all ties of socio-material embodiment, can lead to true enlightenment by which there is final release.

And in all these traditions, however differently interpreted, the role of body-determining and soul-binding *karm*a is crucial. Each particular life-embodiment is determined by the inescapable karmic cycle of action and the fruit of action. Even in the most body-positive perception of the Vaiṣṇavas, *karma* (though said to be God-controlled) brings in an element of ambiguity for creation and the embodying process, as well as for the controlling role of God.

None of the above is intended as criticism that cannot be equally applied to Christian tradition. Nor should we forget the changes in interpretation within any tradition that take place through the ages. The fundamental point being made here is merely that the probably over-optimistic perception of the human body by which we have been conditioned in the modern age is not that found in virtually every religious tradition.

As for primal traditions, while they are so closely earth-related, they also usually include, as we noted, various disciplines for the body – such as the deliberate endurance of pain or deprivation perhaps as an initiatory rite. No tradition, therefore, seems to be without some degree of body-ambivalence. And does this not reflect what is in fact experienced in our life as embodied beings, in the fullest sense of 'embodiment' – individual, social, cosmic? However much modernity may expect perfect health, freedom from all want, unimpeded self-expression, the sense of being perfectly at ease in one's body, the reality will remain one of ambivalence at some point in the inclusive body's experience. Such realism is in fact demanded if we are to take the God-given process of our embodiment seriously. Such realism is not a contradiction of, but a confirming of, the belief that our body-experience can potentially be 'epiphanic'.

The Role of Symbol & Image: Eliade's Influence

More than any other scholar in Religions, it was Mircea Eliade who helped to recover the vital role of images and symbols in religious life. Those looking for a more hard-edged empirically descriptive approach to religious phenomena find Eliade's Jungian-style ontological commitments methodologically inadequate. Even so, his analysis of the phenomenon of symbolism[22] has been very important for our understanding of how symbols function.

Of the six motifs Eliade enumerates, we will note only the following:

(i) He points to the *multivalent* character of symbols; multiple meanings being expressed through one symbol, even at the same time. (ii) And this allows human consciousness, in its deciphering and systematizing role, to discover, through such multivalence, meanings that can be integrated into a world-view. (iii) Thus, symbols are able to express paradox and structures of reality and sacrality otherwise inexpressible. Ours is the creative task of articulating unitive meaning. (iv) Though symbols will always disclose realities inter-relating with actual existential situations in life, translating them into cosmological terms and thus unveiling the structures of reality – as symbols are translated into concepts – bring new meaning into that human existence.[23]

In view of this understanding of symbols, and the preceding discussion concerning the specific role of body-imagery in religious traditions, let me now propose five theses regarding the way in which our religious images relate to our belief-systems, our theological concepts.

Religious Imagery and Belief-Systems

1. The *potent matrix* of religious life lies in its *imagery* – its symbols, signs and sacraments, its parables and pictures, metaphors and analogies, models and paradigms. However, these last two types of imagery assume the emergence, even the conscious selection, of a dominant *controlling image* from within one's faith-world. Thus 'body' has become just such a controlling image in the theology of Rāmānuja, and in important strands of Christian theology.
2. These images emerge essentially out of the *shared experience of the community of faith*, which is often the shared experience of the *wider human community*. In other words, our faith imagery is born out of both the peculiar 'salvation-history' of the faith-community (for Christians this is focussed in the Jesus-story), and the wider, often overlapping, human experience of shared earth-life, and thus the corporate memories that are thrust up in our consciousness as a result of this. Our humanness provides the grounding for our Christianness, though – for people of faith

– the latter provides the specific dynamic for the former. The body-image points very clearly to this dialectic: the 'body of Christ' and the basic human experience of embodiment are crucial for faith, making this eminently appropriate as a 'controlling' and 'epiphanic' image for life.

3. While doctrinal systems and conceptual theory do not provide the essential dynamic of faith, such *conceptualising* is, nevertheless, an *essential part of the faith-process*, of faith's fabric. For one thing, faith necessarily involves drawing out *meaning* from our vision of God. And meaning will necessarily be in relation to life-context. This is what *theo-logia* is all about: interpreting the images of faith so that meaning is experienced in changing contexts and the inherent threat of such change is overcome. Without interpretation, images – though pregnant with the memory of past meaning – cannot give birth to living faith. Contexts compel concepts; thus, image-based theology of some kind is inescapable. And so the image of the body becomes an inclusive 'body' of belief. Indeed, a convincing and inclusive *credo* can be developed based on the image of the body, as I have recently attempted.[24]

4. Images must always be allowed their *multivalent* character, and thus their potency to lead on to new meaning. If a favoured interpretation prevents further insight and the emergence of a wider 'body of belief', we are guilty of fossilising and thus of absolutising a particular perception of an icon, and so trying to limit God, which is the idolatry the prophets condemn. The 'body', as a basic image, points us in numerous directions as faith seeks meaningful expression. Even that body on the cross carries the potency for a wide range of atonement doctrines, none of which exhaust the fullness of meaning of the passion of Jesus (and some of which even seem contrary to key elements in the Gospel story).

What, though, of the claim that any image of faith holds within it such paradox of meaning that conceptual 'opposites' (the *coincidentiae oppositorum* of classical theology) are possible, even necessary to the task of understanding the Object of faith? The answer is that 'paradox' does not mean innate contradiction. The eucharistic 'body of Christ' is, for example, both a real presence and is still earth-grown bread, whatever further theory we may adopt – transubstantiation, consubstantiation, etc – to explain this paradox. The ecclesial 'body of Christ' is very much a human, and therefore error-prone, institution, as well as being a sacred community. These are paradoxical meanings.

Need for Coherence as well as Paradox

Yet, the compulsions of the need for inner coherence are evident here. The human experience of the 'body' may well range so widely, though surely errantly, as to include clear contradictions and self-destructiveness. Even so, both in our eco-embodiment and in the particularity of the Christ-ecclesia-embodiment, there are innate compulsions within the body-image which for faith exerts certain controls on the meaning to be found in that body-imagery – or in any imagery embedded in faith-traditions. Image and concept are to bear innate correspondence if the true potency of the image is to be the basis for a meaning-system.

There are obvious examples of this: Christians have been made aware that their internal divisions contradict their being as the 'one body of Christ'. Similarly, while traditionally there was no doubt an organic economic and even ritual interdependence between the various castes within Indian society, the graded system of the pure and polluted also seemingly at the heart of that system can never seriously be made compatible with the image of that society as a 'body'.

Here, though, we find the Apostle Paul, in using the body-image, referring to 'members' whose functions 'seem weaker' perhaps less 'honourable', than others, but are all equally parts of the one body, i.e. Christ. Yet, he fiercely affirms, all are equal: 'Slaves or free…there is no division in the body; all have the same concern for one another. If one part of the body suffers, all parts suffer with it… '(1Cors.12). In fact, it was along these lines that I often concluded when I'd been invited to speak to Vaiṣṇavas about their tradition and its vision of the world as a divine body: 'Discrimination against any who are, in your own vision of things, part of the one divine body, is surely an unacceptable contradiction?'

No Concept-Free Image

5. Such is the inter-penetration of image and concept that, just as there is no such thing as 'pure reason' in theology, so there is no such thing as a *concept-free image*. When an artist depicts the cross, or the body of Christ either as suffering or risen, when poetry or story includes imagery, meaning is always communicated along with the art, the poetry, the story. Artist, poets, myth-makers are theologising too, at least in so far as they focus on images of faith. The difference is that, because the meaning of their images remains less explicit and systematic, this leaves those who see and read and hear free to share in the process of meaning-communication. So, at the close of one of his most potent parables, Jesus says, 'if you have ears to hear, then hear.'[25] Along with artists and poets, Jesus too ministered on the boundaries between image and concept, at the point where meaning remains most potent.

Creative Juxtaposing of Images in Arts and Religion

6. In art, poetry and story-telling, it is often the creative juxtaposing of images that provides originality and impact. And this raises the question of how images relate to each other, as they obviously are made to in conceptual systems. Religious traditions invariably incorporate a coherence within which one key-image controls the role, even the meaning, of the others. A prioritising of images takes place in this process of discovering meaning.

Thus, in the Vedānta of Rāmānuja, although we find much of the same basic material as Śaṅkara deals with, the resulting system is not a mere 'modifying' of Advaita (as Neo-Vedāntins usually claim). Rather, the Advaitic vision is turned upside-down.

And this is done by placing the body-image at the centre, allowing this image to determine ontological and epistemological, as well as the more obvious cosmological and soteriological priorities. Relationality ('inseparable relationship'[26] to use Rāmānuja's term treasured by his tradition), innate to the body-image, became the dominant visionary centre-point.

In this way, for Rāmānuja the body-image functioned as a paradigmatic model. Other images cluster around this central image, their function and meaning being determined by it. There is imagery of Master-servant, King-subject, Leader-led; of technical terms such as *prakāra-prakārī, śeṣa-śeṣī;* there are many of the common images of Vedānta such as light, chariot, lake, lotus and many more; there are the divinised Vedic images of Fire, Wind, Sky, Earth, Waters, etc. But, while we should certainly not underplay the role of key God-images depicting the greatness and majesty, as well as the intimacy of God, in the end all these images take their meaning from the controlling image of everything related to God as a body to its inner Self. It is this *deha-dehī-bhāva* that shapes Rāmānuja's style of relational Vedānta.

Conclusion: Need for Cross-Cultural Engagement

By way of conclusion, some comments at a time of crisis in Christian mission, a time when those who work in any way at the frontiers between peoples of different faiths need far more sensitive understanding of each other. It should be fairly obvious to readers that such understanding is far from the ulterior motive of acquiring the skill to convert the other to 'our way of believing'.

(a) In the first place we need far more informed recognition of the potent role of imagery in all human communication. It is not merely that we need more art and poetry. All involved in cross-cultural situations, whatever their particular vocation, need insight into the dynamics of image and concept within faith-systems.

(b) Because images invariably emerge from within the life of an indigenous culture, those on such 'mission' boundaries must also be aware that the meaning initially communicated by any image will be conditioned by the perceptions of that local culture.

Such tacit meanings will speak more loudly than the explicit meanings we assume are being communicated.

(c) In the movement from one culture and its faith to another, therefore, three compelling questions emerge:

(i) What are the common basic images shared between people of differing faiths who nevertheless are rooted in a common culture, common because of shared humanness, and therefore necessarily shared primal images of life? Is not body-imagery, arising from shared experience of embodiment, one such pivotal point of convergence?

(ii) Even within the scriptures of Christian tradition is there not a re-locating of the 'controlling images' of faith? The central kingdom-image of some gospels (e.g. Matthew), for example, is replaced by the cross, or by the body, or by other primal images such as light, water, etc, (e.g. in John) depending on the need for *meaning* within particular contexts. Cultural context makes all the difference to the way faith is understood.

(iii) Are there new and distinctive images in the cultural context, not perhaps found within the Judeo-Christian tradition, which can become faith-enhancing images for Christians? There is, for example, the drum, found in many primal traditions as an instrument of epiphanic power. Significant is Sathi Clarke's recent exploration of the meaning of the drum, especially as an instrument of resistance to caste dominance over the social body in the life of the 'Drum people' (Paraiyars) of Tamil Nadu, and as a way into a Drummer Christology. Or, we may think of the cock in Kashi tradition, which Jyoti Sahi has reflected on in a series of paintings. Or, there is the 'rice theology' of the Far East, and the 'coconut theology' of which Pacific Islanders have spoken. These images not only provide insight into traditional cultural traditions; in looking at Christian faith by way of such imagery, new and needed insights can be drawn from that faith, just as the images themselves also take on new meaning in this process of interchange. Such inter-penetration, in other words, can prove mutually fruitful.

A 'Critical' Perspective also needed

Nor can a critical perspective be left out as we mutually explore our imagery. Indeed, the painful life-experience of some will make that critical perspective an inescapable starting point. Body-imagery is so bound up with community, with national existence, with self-identity – its culture, its economy, its spirituality – that in India there can be no avoiding the burning issue of caste in general and the status of Dalits in particular. Mission – pushing out one's body-boundaries, seeking to bring greater wholeness to the wider body, whether in the name of Christ or of all humanity with its imprinted divine image – will necessarily become critically involved in questions of caste. In terms of the Ṛg Veda's ancient image of the body of the sacrificed Person, who are really to constitute the serving feet, the mobile thighs, the strong shoulders, the word-empowered mouth, of the emergent community? Who actually purifies, who pollutes? And how is power to be shared in this all-inclusive community-body if it is to survive as one?

Yet mission can never be a one-way process. Any person of faith standing between two cultures who does not learn (from God) in the experience and thus from the indigenous culture of the 'other', is one who is not faithful to the gospel of Word-become-flesh. Nor can we omit the (literally) *crucial* factor in that Word-become-flesh faith – viz. the suffering and crucifying of the enfleshed One. Faith of this embodied One calls for the denial of self, and a life lived in the service of others – another key factor in the recovery of God's creation.

In that the greatest single ideological challenge to global Christian mission is its minimal credibility to date on the issue of the human relationship to nature, it is precisely in this area of eco-theology that primal imagery can make, and is already making, maximum impact. Earth's body, the creation-body of God, can yet be healed and renewed. But it is not the dominant imagery of *western* Judeo-Christian missionary vision that will effect this.

Endnotes

1. Cf. my *Vision, Tradition, Interpretation*, Berlin: Mouton de Gruyter 1988, especially chapters 2-3, 5-7.
2. E.g. Ṛg Veda 10.90, the Puruṣa Śūkta.
3. I have written in much greater detail on this theme elsewhere: e.g. *God and the Universe in the Vedāntic Theology of Rāmānuja*, Madras: Rāmānuja Research Society, 1976; *Vedāntic Approaches to God*, London: Macmillan 1980; 'Rāmānuja's *Śarīra-Śarīrī-Bhāva:* A Conceptual Analysis' in *Studies in Rāmānuja*, Madras: Rāmānuja Vedānta Centre 1980.
4. A theme I have explored in detail in chapter six above; an earlier version was The Mythic Symbol Avatāra in Indian Conceptual Formulations', *Dialogue and Alliance*, Vol. 1, No. 2, 1987, pp. 3-12.
5. A comment on Pillai Lokacarya's *Tattva Traya* III. 202, quoted by M. Yamunacharya in *Viśiṣṭādvaita: Philosophy and Religion*, Madras: Rāmānuja Research Society 1974, p. 208.
6. E.g. H. Eilberg-Schwartz, 'God's Body: The Divine Cover-up', in *Religious Reflections on the Human Body,* Edit. J. M. Law, Indianapolis: Indiana University Press 1995. With eight essays on Buddhist and Far-eastern religious traditions, there is a bewildering lack of treatment of Hinduism, with the exception of one essay on a contemporary Guru. Yet there are two chapters on Islam.
7. E.g. Ephs.2.14; Hebs.10.10; I Pet.2.24; Jn.1-14.

7a. In *Healing Wings: Acts of Jesus for Human Wholeness* (with collaboration by artist Jyoti Sahi and poet Jane Sahi), 1st edit. Bangalore 1998; 2nd edition Leicester 2014. There I reflect at a popular level on the meaning of 16 healing acts of Jesus.

8. Roms.12; I Cors.12; Ephs.1.23; Ephs.4; Cols.1.18; 24; 2.19. John Robinson's *The Body: A Study in Pauline Theology*, London: SCM 1957, is still an essay of great importance.
9. Cols. 1.15-20.
10. This is elaborated in a very early essay of mine, 'Anointing and Ministry in the New Testament', *Indian Journal of Theology*, Vol. 16, Nos. 1-2, 1967, pp. 137-52.
11. Cf. e.g. *Ecotheology: Voices from South and North*, edit. D G Hallman, Geneva: WCC 1994; *Ecology: A Theological Response*, Madras: Gurukul 1994. There is, though, little, if any explicit reference to creation as God's body in these two books.
12. Cf. the writings of Charles Hartshorne and John Cobb.
13. Cf. Anne Hunt Overzee, *The Body Divine: The Symbol of the Body in the Works of Teilhard de Chardin and Rāmānuja,* Cambridge: CUP 1992. Essential reading for further focus on a number of the issues raised in this essay.
14. Cf. e.g. Matthew Fox's *Original Blessing*, Santa Fe Bear and Co, 1983.

15. Especially the writings of Sally McFague: e.g. 'Imaging a Theology of Nature: The World as God's Body', in Birch, Eakin and McDaniel, eds. *Liberating Life*, New York: Orbis 1990.
16. E.g. Christopher Duraisingh. And the writing, in an earlier generation, of Bishop A. J. Appasamy should also be noted (See B.P. Dunn's fine study, *A.J. Appasamy and his Reading of Rāmānuja: A Comparative Study in Divine Embodiment*, Oxford 2016).
17. A recent editorial in *Dalit Voice* disparaged all ecological exhortations as further attempts by oppressors and western capitalists to hoodwink the exploited third world.
18. Cf. e.g. K. C. Abraham's comment in *Ecotheology,* pp. 65-66. 'There is a growing awareness of the organic link between the destruction of the environment and social, economic and political justice'. (See also the essay following below in this collection, 'Changing Eco-faith Perspectives in India').
19. E.g. Roms. 8.1-13. Note how the Greek term *sarx* (usually 'flesh') is variously translated in modern versions.
20. Roms. 7.24.
21. Even the body of creation has this longing for renewal: Roms. 8.19-21.
22. M. Eliade, *Images and Symbols: Studies in Religious Symbolism*, New York: Sheed and Ward 1961.
23. A fuller summary is found in *Vision, Tradition, Interpretation*, pp. 123-125.
24. In *Ultimate Visions*, edit. M Forward, Oxford: One World Books, pp. 184-85.
25. Mk. 4.9.
26. *Dalits and Christianity: Subaltern Religion and Liberation Theology in South India*, OUP Delhi, 1998.

8

Changing Eco-Faith Perspectives in India

Even up to the late 1980s eco-attitudes in theological circles in India were very different from today. The response of a professor at a seminar in Bangalore on socio-economic issues I helped organise in 1985 remains vividly in my memory: 'Your eco-concerns merely reflect the leisure-concerns and vested interests of an affluent West. Economic justice for the poor is the only possible priority in India today'. And this met with approval by most of those present – theologians, sociologists, social activists and ethicists. Thirty years later attitudes contrast dramatically with this economic reductionism.

My own conversion to an eco-faith was much earlier. Long convinced that theological concern without 'eco-concern' at its centre can have little to do with true 'God-talk' (or *Theo-logy*), it was around the late 1970s that this latent eco-faith became more explicit in my writing. For it was then I realised that there is an inescapable ecological dimension to human need, that eco-cultural analysis has to be an integral part of any convincing social and economic analysis, and that this eco-dimension of faith, an 'eco-vision', is most imperative within the Indian cultural and theological context.[1]

Latin-American liberationist thought seriously neglected this eco-cultural dimension in its early years. Socio-economic analysis was seen as sufficiently radical. And this was the radicalism taken over by Indian liberationists in the 1970-80s. Yet it is only when socio-economic analysis includes an ecological thrust that the most inclusively radical account of India's poverty and oppression becomes possible.

Passion for our '*oikos*', our 'house/home', is at the heart of this new radicalism. *Oiko-nomos* (economics) concerns the just ordering of material resources within the human 'household'. *Oiko-logia* (ecology) can, but does not always, probe deeper to the roots, i.e. to the 'radical' sources, of the prevalent unjust ordering, by seeking to re-order our whole human embodiment. It is not only the domestic arrangements we make for intra-human economics that will ensure a just ordering of things. The broader scope of a new earth-relationship is called for; we need a radically new vision of our inter-relations with the habitat from which every resource for human development, indeed every resource for being human at all, originates. There can be no just economy without a re-visioning of our relations with the world that gives us our embodiment.

Mere Conservationism?

Any such eco-faith will still no doubt need a strong injection of socialist economic analysis. For environmental concern can easily lose its radical edge by becoming a conservationism of the elite, focussing solely on habitat, with little recognition of the human presence in that habitat. Like every other movement, ecology can be manipulated by conservative forces. Indeed, the earlier third-world rejection of the eco-faith that I (having come from the West) preached was understandable. Much environmentalist sermonising from the West used to be from a thoroughly elitist perspective: 'Cut down your population' (Because if you consume as much as we Westerners do, there are global resources only for a fraction of the world's population); 'Clean up your toilet habits' (Though you will have to learn to do so without using the volume of water we do; there certainly is not sufficient tappable water for you to wash toilets, bodies, dishes, clothes, cars, to sprinkle lawns and fill swimming pools, in the way we do); 'Stop felling your trees' (or there will be no hardwood left for our furniture); 'Do not increase your use of vehicles and consumer goods that pollute the atmosphere' (We have already polluted it enough to cause global warming); 'Join the nuclear non-proliferation pact' (We Big Four have already sufficiently endangered the continued existence of the world); 'Protect the tiger, the elephant, the rhino' (so that our tourists can still come to enjoy the sight of these exotic species).

The parenthetical afterthoughts in the above may usually have been far from the thinking of many western environmentalists; but so much of this hectoring from afar seemed to others to carry the message: What right do you Third-world developing nations think you have to enjoy the indulgent consumerist life-style that we've developed for ourselves?

I should not, then, have been greatly surprised at the often cynical dismissal by Indian radical theologians of my perhaps feeble attempts from the late-1970s to incorporate an eco-dimension into the growing liberationist movement. Indeed, the extraordinary burgeoning of ecological awareness among both Indian intellectuals and grass-root activists since the mid-1980s does not greatly surprise me. Such an awareness was, I felt even then, latent there all the time, as one of the editorials I wrote for *Bangalore Theological Forum* indicates:[2]

> The more inclusive world-views of at least some (Indian) cultures which perceive human life as dynamically nurtured by and organically participant in earth's life, are still living *darśanas*, dynamic factors in people's consciousness. Christian theological reflection within these cultural contexts cannot but make an essential contribution to the needed global eco-vision.

Reasons for Change of Perception

A number of reasons can be listed for the recent and rapid change in overt perception of how important eco-matters are: 1) There is the almost apocalyptic speed and intrusive scale of the signs of ecological crisis in India.

2) Within India's diversity of cultural life – from Adivasi to the various forms of vernacular and Sanskritic culture – there is a wide range of pro-earth factors, intuitive cultural values and indigenous attitudes that provide potential resources for the emergence of a conscious critique of eco-destructive ways of life.

3) Then there is the long tradition in India of critical reflection on the relationship between the conscious self and the natural world. The experiential raw materials underlying this reflective process, in all its diversity, were deeply indigenous. This means that even though the *darśanas* emerging from such reflection were sometimes quite elitist (Yoga, Vedānta, etc.), they embody perceptions – metaphysical, moral, spiritual – that are deeply embedded in the psyche of large sections of Indian society.

4) Of more specific contemporary significance, there is the fact that India has been blessed in recent times with a number of outstandingly perceptive and articulate socio-cultural analysts and local activists for whom the integration of socio-economics and habitat concern has been imperative. We might note such widely varied expressions of this have been found in Anil Agarwal, Sunderlal Bahuguna, Jayanto Bandopadhyay, Madhav Gadgil, Ramachandra Guha, Rajni Kothari, Ashis Nandi, Vandana Shiva as but a few names among many.[3]

5) And, of course, the ecological issue has become inescapably *global*. All the empirical evidence compels us to acknowledge that it is not merely a fad or a foible of the affluent.

Whatever ecological awareness there may now be in India among academics and local activists alike, to what extent can we say that *theological awareness* and articulation has even kept pace with this 'perceptual shift', let alone provided prophetic pointers to give direction to the 'secular' world in this matter?

Ecology as Interconnectedness

Ecology is all about linkages, the interconnectedness of things. Eco-logy is the science of our *oikos*-ness, the systematic investigation of habitat-systems, and of how humans interact with this habitat, with the bio-systems that sustain them. This *oikos* which is our habitat is our mother's 'house with many rooms', each of which is an eco-system linked in subtle but functionally organic ways with all the other myriad rooms of our global home. Merely smoke a cigarette (leave alone kill off a whole species with a pesticide) in one 'room' and the fumes, in some subtle way, will touch the life of every other 'room'. Equally innate to the whole *oikos*, though, are seemingly infinite powers of adaptation even if this entails shedding massive numbers of life-forms. Linkage, then, is the name of the game in our eco-world.

This is the main reason for the critique by ecological visionaries – including Greens, New Agers, Eco-feminists, New Internationalists – of many of the assumptions of modern techno-scientific method. An important ingredient of the European 'Enlightenment' was the sharp *dichotomy between mind and nature*, with Bacon and Descartes as crucial fathers of this mind-set that emerged in the early scientific movement in the 16th and 17th centuries. Nature was believed to have been set free from the constraints of her prior sacral status. And 'man', as the instrument of mind's transcendence, was believed to have been set free for unfettered exploring of nature's powers, and to unlimited exploiting of nature's resources, made amply available for human benefit. In this engineering and exploiting of nature's latent powers lay, it was believed, a wonderful future for the human race, or at least for those privileged races able to direct this process.

It was not until the 19th century that techno-science advanced to the point of beginning to make its full impact on industrial development. By then the colonising of Asia, Africa, Australia and the Americas had reached its zenith. That the exploitation of peoples (especially non-Europeans, but not exclusively so; the 'workers' and 'weaker' were exploited everywhere), and the exploitation their countries' resources that accompanied the exploitation of nature should not surprise us. The whole of this phenomenon of the modern period of human history is essentially based on the *control*, especially the technological control, of the 'undeveloped' environment, whether nature or humans. In fact, a vocabulary of violence as the method of development seemed quite proper to Bacon when referring in the very early stages of the

Industrial Age to the human task of conquering nature. She was to be 'mastered', 'beaten into' submission. This was a mind-nature dichotomy with a vengeance.

Precisely the opposite is what ecology sees as the 'connectedness' of the whole eco-system of which humans are an integral part. No wonder, then, that there has been a stream of anti-science from 'deep-green' environmentalists. In view of the historical and ideological linkage, sad but undeniable, between the established churches, with their colonising and industrialising power-linkages, and the dichotomous attitude to nature often expressed by western Christian writers (at least until very recently), no wonder too that Christian faith is in the West identified by the Green movement generally as 'anti-earth'.

Along with all religious systems, then, Christian theology too has much to learn from this ecological movement, especially in so far as it is linked integrally with the concern for economic justice as suggested above. At last that linkage is increasingly being made in Indian theological discourse. The late K.C.Abraham was among the first (in 1994) to express this dawning realisation clearly:[4]

> Our problem, it was assumed, was poverty and economic exploitation; the environmental issue was a 'luxury' of the industrialised countries. Social action groups and people's movements in Third World countries thus showed relative indifference to the problem of ecology. Today, we realize how urgent this issue is for the whole world... there is a growing awareness of the organic link between the destruction of the environment and social, economic and political injustice. The interconnectedness between commitment to the renewal of society and to the renewal of the earth is clearly seen in the struggle of many marginalized groups all over the world.

If Christian theology, and Indian theology in particular, is to make a positive impact upon the ecological movement – instead of being suspect as anti-earth – there are so many ways in which new, further linkages are to be made. These are in part based on insights from the ecological movement itself, as Christian faith interacts with its ideological thrust. For, the eco-faith I envision is no merely uncritical imitation of secular ecology; and whereas ecology and economy belong intrinsically and integrally together, the linkages I propose here may at first appear to be mutually exclusive polarities. They are not; for only through their creative interaction can new forms of eco-faith emerge.

Listing the Linkages

1. We begin with the crucial linkage of (literally) down-to-earth *empirical realism* and *cosmic vision.* Eco-faith needs both:

(a) *Fact-based Research:* We need the hard-edged, fact-based, micro-research, focussed on specific instances of the effect of human behaviour on the immensely complex eco-systems we relate to. Such empirical research has already resulted in the accumulation of a massive amount of data recording how our habitat functions, and what we have done to that habitat.[5] Often it is not only highly technical; it makes for depressing, gloom-and-doom reading, though there are also points of optimism as the growing number of small-scale environmentalist development bodies (a notable feature of Indian life) make their impact locally. Theological reflection must be grounded firmly in such systematic research, if our eco-theology is to achieve public credibility. Even students in first-level theological courses need at least to be introduced to this material describing the eco-damage of our times.

(b) *And a visionary dimension:* No religious reflection or theology, however, can ever be solely a deductive process, arriving at conclusions entirely on the basis of empirically-established data. We begin, as in all religious traditions, with vision – in this case with eco-vision. 'If there is no vision', said the early Hebrew prophet, 'the people perish'. And in the modern world, certainly much of creation will perish too, without eco-vision.

It is lamentable that Christian theology has taken so long to place ecological issues at the centre of its reflection. This awakening seems to have come about only when – as a result of industrialisation, deforestation, market-oriented agricultural policies, and various other aspects of our modern life-style – the world has reached ecological crisis-point obvious to all except the few with vested interests at stake. Is it only when there is irrefutable evidence of massive air, water and food pollution, of destructive soil-erosion and consequent silting, flooding, or its opposite, desertification, when there is the threat of global warming or loss of fuel resources or of famine – is it only then that theologians put ecology on their agenda?

Would this have been the case if we had been gripped by a basic and inclusive vision that 'the earth and all her fullness is God's' (to use the words of the ancient Hebrew singer), directly deriving from and throbbing with the life of the creative Source and End of all life? Admittedly, the plea for vision still leaves us with the problem of how this inner perception comes to grips with the hard empirical realities of that human activity by which we relate to our habitat. But, with a truly living faith in our creaturely realm as pregnant with divine purpose, as exalted by the divine evaluation, 'It is good,'[6] how is it possible not to foresee, prophetically, that a callous exploitative attitude on the part of technology-empowered humans is going to be disastrous?

Need for compelling eco-vision: Such a vision entails a compelling passion for the whole creaturely world, whatever hard compromises may be entailed in the establishing of our human habitat within that wider *oikos*. There is no way humans can live in total non-violent harmony with all other creatures, however much we may hope for such inter-creaturely harmony in the *Eschaton*. Such visionary faith in creation has, as we have seen, to be grounded in the findings of empirical realists. And yet, in the end what will compel us is only an eco-vision that transcends our data and our documentation. The theological process is always that, in the final analysis, of drawing out the meaning of our primary vision.[7]

For Christians, as much as for theistic Hindus, their vision of God has necessarily to include a *cosmic* dimension. God, and the God-human relationship, must always include a God-creation and a human-creation dimension. Concern for the freedom and transcendence of God raised in the theologically orthodox the anxiety of making God dependent on creation, or of making creation necessary to God (a problem struggled with in both Christian and Hindu classical theological traditions). God can surely take care of her/his own independence. A far greater threat is to perceive creation as somehow independent of God, and to perceive of our human relationship to God as somehow not intrinsically incorporating our relationship with creation. ('Incorporating' is a key word here, but I will take its fuller meaning up later). We are, in our essential ontological being, earthlings. This is a primary image we need of ourselves.

Vision and imagination belong together. This means that one crucial way of inspiring and sustaining an eco-vision is the image-focussing, image-creating work of artists and poets. Their imagery is just as important, perhaps more important because more creative, than the empirical data of eco-scientists. In my own eco-faith journey I have found many of the paintings of Jyoti Sahi outstandingly evocative, drawing as he does on primal (often explicitly 'tribal') imagery of our earth-life.[8] In many instances he depicts natural phenomena – rocks, hills, trees, pools, rivers – as communicating a divine 'presence'. Traditional theological fears that such immanentalism threatens the immutability of God seem to me to contradict the central modes of embodying self-expression by which God's presence comes close to us, viz., creation and incarnation.

Both these two, then – eco-vision and empirical realism – in their mutual interaction, need each other.

Talk of ontological 'vision' brings to mind the *darśana* tradition of India, the Vedantic theological visionary insights in particular. The question is, as a Christian eco-faith seeks resources for its articulation, do these Indian visionary systems provide significant input, even a viable visionary framework, for our reflecting on the meaning of our eco-life? Certainly many in the Green movement in the West, as part of a 'New Age' approach to reality, having lost faith in what they see as the exclusive, patriarchal and aggressive monotheism of the western Christian tradition, now claim to find a more convincing holistic vision in

Indian religion and culture. We shall look at the implications of this claim in our next section.

Interaction of Biblical Faith and Wider Cultural Life

2. The second crucial linkage is this: the *creative interaction of biblical faith with wider religio-cultural traditions of the human community*. Biblical eco-faith, in the eyes of many ecologically sensitive writers, is almost a contradiction in terms. In particular, the creation story of Genesis 1 has in recent years been the target of fierce criticism, and not only from eco-feminists. The main focus for this is the command to Adam to 'have dominion over the earth' and her creatures, and to 'fill the earth' with the human presence. Lynn White, for example, argued as long ago as 1967 that this text was the cause of Christians having to bear a 'huge burden of guilt' for the devastation earth's life has suffered at the hands of those who justified their violent domination of earth and earth's peoples, on the grounds of this divine command. White's stricture has been repeated by ecological writers again and again. Generally speaking it is a sad fact that Christian faith stands abysmally low in the esteem of eco-exponents. White himself, incidentally, believed that it was not Christian faith per se that was to be condemned, but a particular hermeneutic that legitimated eco-destruction. The Franciscan form of Christian faith, for example, he saw as eminently eco-friendly.

Re-examining Our Creation Stories

Is there, then, a more ecologically acceptable, as well as exegetically valid, interpretation of the biblical story of creation? Already in the telling of the first (priestly?) Genesis story (Gen.1), as in virtually all creation-significant passages throughout the bible, there is interaction with other religio-cultural tradition. In re-shaping the Babylonian material the Genesis story-teller clearly aims to emphasise the following:

(a) It is *God* alone from whom all creaturely life derives, and by whom order emerges from chaos. (b) It is the powerful, purposeful *Word*, the trans-material self-articulation of God that effects this creative process. (c) Creaturely life is, in the purpose of God, essentially and originally `*good*' (several times repeated). (d) Human life is the *crown* of this creative process. (e) Humans, bearing the *Creator's likeness* in a special way, are commissioned to carry out the divine rule on earth. (Incidentally, as part of overseeing, in this early biblical story, though not subsequent to Fall and Flood, humans were expected to be vegetarian!)

Two significant features of the second (Gen. 2 and probably earlier creation story) are that humans are made literally from the earth, by divine inbreathing, and they are to 'care for' the (garden-like) habitat they are placed in. Some other key biblical passages are:

a) The Genesis 9 passage in which, following the flood (another clear parallel with Babylonian mythic material?) God makes a solemn covenant of peace with humans and 'with every living creature'. (Preceding this, however, humans are given freedom to eat meat, and to be a cause of 'dread' to all other creatures. Is it *awe* that is intended here? In any case, God will never again curse the earth because of humans). (b) Numerous Psalms express God's delight in and care for creation, as well as the blessings bestowed on human life through creation (e.g. Palms 65, 67, 72, 104). (c) There are Prophetic passages depicting the promised *Shalom* with all creation (e.g.Isa. 11). (d) There are Jesus-stories, such as his healings and the calming of the storm, suggesting his creation-restoring significance. (e) There are Apostolic passages speaking of the liberation of all creation (e.g. Romans 8) and of the whole of cosmic life being created through Christ and cohering together because of Christ (Colossians 1) and the renewing of the divine image in humanity in and through Christ.

Key-points in a 'Biblical Eco-faith'

In general, we may affirm as 'biblical faith' (recognising too the diversity of vision in scripture) that: (i) the earth and all its life is *God's*, and for this reason is of great worth and destined for great glory. (ii) In God's eternal purpose all creation is *good*, is of intrinsic value (not merely of value to humans) and will yet be perfected in an age of peace and justice. (iii) Humans – especially the 'Last Man' Christ – have a crucial role in the exercising of the divine rule and in realising the divine goal for creation.

Some of these biblical affirmations are usually seen as deeply problematic by many eco-enthusiasts. I will mention three such: 1) That creation is dependent upon the purpose of a *personal* God (especially if depicted in male terms); 2) that Christ has a necessary instrumental role in realising this purpose; and 3) that humans are the *crown* of creation and bear a crucial responsibility for earth's destiny (especially if held to be 'stewards' of creation).

At the outset we have to recognise that there may well be an inescapable clash of vision here. Not all differing viewpoints are reconcilable. But there is also the possibility that it was our culturally-conditioned ways of interpreting biblical faith – especially in view of the impact on biblical scholarship of western techno-science, with all its presuppositions – that prevented the full range of creation's meaning from emerging in our Christian faith-talk.

Dialogical Inter-play

It was precisely in the interpretative encounter of Yahweh-faith (and Christ-faith) with the cultural worlds of Canaan, Babylon, and then the Mediterranean, that these distinctive biblical emphases on creation began to be affirmed. Why on earth should we imagine that this interactive process must not continue – in new cultural environments? Why should we not expect that God will shape for us new ways of perceiving creation, as well as other aspects of faith, as we engage in this continuing interaction? Certainly for me, the very words, 'In the beginning, God created', have already acquired various new nuances of meaning as a result of dialogical interplay both with key Hindu theological traditions, where similar phrases often occur, as well as with various non-classical, more obviously primal, traditions.

That word 'interplay' provides a clue here. The Indian way of imaging creation in terms of 'play' (*līlā*) and dance (*naṭa*), of an overflowing of God's creative being in an unrestrained and spontaneous playfulness that brings no particular benefit to the Creator – this image now inevitably comes to mind for me whenever it is affirmed that 'God created'.

No single 'Indian' view of Creation

There are, of course, so many other ways of imaging and interpreting creation in the Indic traditions with which biblical faith is to interact. There is no single uniform *darśana* undergirding Indian religio-cultural life, in spite of claims to this effect by neo-Vedantins and ultra-Hindu nationalists.

However, this fact of serious ontological diversity raises an important question both for biblical faith as it seeks dialogical partners, and for eco-visionaries in the West who see in Eastern religion a world-view less exclusive and aggressive than that which they see in the Western Christian tradition. Both have to realise that within Indian religio-cultural history there has, for at least a millennium, been a vigorous struggle between two opposite ontological positions – the Realists and the Transcendentalists. It has been a struggle between those who, whatever commitment they may have to Other Being, were adamant that cosmic life and creaturely experience is ultimately real; and those who, whatever concessionary, provisional reality they allow to creation's existence, in the end could not allow that such dependent, changing existence was ultimately real.

It was especially among the Vedāntic *darśanas* that this struggle was most fierce and most theologically articulate. Theistic Vedāntins mounted a spirited attack in responding to Advaitic teaching (that followed the lead of the later Buddhist, Nagarjuna) that there are two levels of being (ontology) and certainly of seeing (epistemology) – i.e. the absolute (*pāramārthika*) and the relative (*vyāvahārika*) – which, by the powerfully delusive role of *māyā* and *avidyā*, is mistakenly experienced as real. In key passages expounding Hindu scripture, Rāmānuja, for example, argued that the whole of creation shares in the being of its Creator, and therefore is ultimately real, vibrant with reflected glory. God is the inner Self, inseparably related to, though distinct from all creaturely beings, which are dependent on and controlled by God just like a body relates to, depends on and is controlled by its self within. Rāmānuja even argued that the words we use for every mundane object in the end denote the Creator, the supreme self of all.[9]

This *pan-en-theistic* vision entails a very different ontological discourse from that of Advaita, where all our cosmic and social existence has a strangely ambiguous reality. In Advaita, as Śañkara puts it, all words `turn back', they can do no more than suggest indirectly the Reality beyond all. Transcendent vision overwhelms our earthiness. Whatever other problems may accompany the vision of the Bhakti-Vedantins (a deeply entrenched socio-religious conservatism in some, for example), they certainly provide significant insights for an eco-vision today. In the transcendentalism of Advaita there is no ultimately real linkage of vision and empirical realism, between ultimacy and earthiness. When we turn, therefore, to Indian cultural traditions for an eco-visionary framework, we have to be critically discriminating. Metaphysical theory does matter; a world-view is inescapable. And the way we ontologically and cosmologically frame that world-view is crucial if it is to be an eco-sensitive world-view. Our dialogical interaction needs to be sustained and rigorous, however open to insights from all sources.[10]

Ultimate Significance in our 'Embodiedness'

3. The third linkage I would propose arises out of the above. If the experience of embodiedness provides a potent image of how divine life relates to cosmic life, then our eco-faith needs to include a linkage of our personal experience of embodiment and a sense of cosmic `bodiedness'. Several Indian traditions, in addition to the Vaiṣṇava tradition, do just this, as we have seen in previous essays, to which little more need be added here. The main conviction is that there is an innate correspondence between micro-cosmic and macro-cosmic being, the sources for which have been looked into earlier.

Body-centred Eco-feminist Perceptions

It is no mere co-incidence that in almost all human culture Nature has been understood as female; that modern scientific technology and the destruction of nature resulting from this has almost entirely been a male endeavour; that men find it far more difficult than women to be in authentic touch with their feelings, with all that relates most immediately to their bodies; that the male gender has most readily acceded to the cerebral alienation from nature of which Bacon and Descartes were metaphysical fathers.

The title of one eco-feminist theological book, *I am my Body*, by Elizabeth Moltmann, may be regarded by a prominent strand of traditional Vedānta as indicating the ultimate delusion, i.e. that a body's sensory experience and thereby its sense of identity is really the self. This is *deha-ātma-bhrama*, from which delusion we need to be set free. However, many eco-feminist insights on the epiphanic role of the body are close to Rāmānuja's vision, though very differently expressed. In reality, behind Rāmānuja's classically expressed body-vision, or at least as one important stream flowing into it, is the pre-classical insight of primal human cultural experience, in which the body is the primary agent in human communication. And it is to this primality that eco-feminism often traces its antecedents. Rāmānuja, too, was undoubtedly, if unconsciously, drawing on indigenous streams of cultural life and religious vision (the counter-cultural dimensions of the *bhakti* movement itself for example) lying behind his formal Vedantic categories. Primal and folk cultural values and insights are only now beginning to be appreciated as resources for eco-vision.[11]

This body-centred linking of our own and cosmic life is far from merely metaphysical. A number of very practical consequences for life-style flow from this way of thinking. For example, to be more body-conscious, more aware of the health-implications of what we eat and drink, the air we breathe in, the sounds we hear, the space in which we move, the elements we touch – all these factors linking micro-body and macro-body can revolutionise life-style. It is when we are aware that our own bodies replicate cosmic embodiment (and my eco-vision would lead me here to say 'the cosmic embodiment of God') that there is a wider compulsion: that of attuning our own life-style and that of the whole human community to greater harmony with earth's life. It is the whole cosmic body that awaits with eager anticipation the final peace and justice that God has promised.

The Linkage of People and Earth

4. A fourth necessary linkage is that of *people and earth*. One of the key biblical insights referred to in section 2 is the ultimate importance of humans in the divine economy. 'Deep Greens' tend to place the value of creaturely life above that of people. It is, they might argue, sheer human arrogance, especially western arrogance, to claim that humans are the crown of creation; only Judeo-Christian anthropocentrism will claim that animal life and nature are there for human benefit.

Hence, some anti-vivisectionists and those who oppose scientific experimentation on rats, guinea-pigs, monkeys and suchlike animals, (which it is not my intention to defend) have no qualms in placing lethal poison even in tins of baby-food in superstores. Such extremist earth-protectors make their value-system very clear. But there are also elitist conservationists, as well as governments, who have no qualms in evicting whole communities of forest-people from their ancestral homes in the name of creating a people-free nature reserve. To such Adivasi people it seems that they are treated as of less value than Bengal tigers, Gir lions and black rhinos.

This frequent confrontation vitiates a basic insight of the ecological movement, that insight with which I began this essay. The justice, peace and socio-economic well-being we seek for people is linked integrally with the well-being of earth's life. Unless and until people develop new ways of relating to the earth which is our habitat, 'people's development' will remain empty rhetoric. So many of our justice issues, especially issues raised by indigenous peoples, are linked directly to ecological issues. But, in the struggle for justice both for oppressed people and impoverished earth, neither can be placed above the other; both need each other, as Rajni Kothari brilliantly argued in his 'Essay on Poverty and Human Consciousness', in *Growing Amnesia* (New Delhi 1993).

Liberation Theology must continue its focus on people and their basic human needs. But the more we do this, if we can be free from some of the constraints of key pre-suppositions in 'modernity' of what those needs are, why they have arisen, and how they can be met, the more we shall find that the real needs of India's poor are inextricably linked with the need to renew their habitat. The great majority of the concerns now raised by Development workers and Non-Governmental Organisations – now that new, more indigenously framed concepts of 'Development' are emerging – prove to be as much about basic earth-matters and modes of production as strictly about distribution. The criticism made of Trans-National Corporations, globalization programmes and World Bank policy invariably focus as much on ecological as on strictly economic factors. But, as we saw earlier, in reality these two aspects of our *oikos*-life can no longer be rigorously separated; they overlap at so many points.

However important it is to draw industry and commerce into the process of making our modern life-style more eco-friendly (by the use of both penalties and incentives), the most blatant contradiction between ecology and economy arises when ecological decisions are made solely on the basis of market-driven economic factors. With the increased globalising of the Indian economy, instances of this are myriad; but we take up this point in the final section.

Throughout the world, and in many places in India, Adivasi people, whose ancestors lived in the forests with a sustainable economy entirely forest-based, are now being evicted from their ancestral habitat. On the day I write this (16 November 1995), the *Times of India* reports a forest-entry demonstration by the tribal people of South Karnataka, concerning their denial of access into the sanctuary forests of Bandipur and Nagarhole. Their aim, they claim, is merely to collect the 'minor forest products' (leaves, resin, seeds, roots, honey, dead twigs) essential to their economy. This joint tribal agitation is based specifically on what they perceive as the State's unwillingness to implement the pro-tribal findings and recommendations of the D. S. Bhuria committee. One recommendation was that Karnataka tribal villages and surrounding forests and waters should be designated as 'scheduled areas', allowing various limited right to tribals over the forest's natural resources. Without total control, however, the Government feels that the immense commercial value of the forests, both in wood, including hardwoods and other greatly valued tree-species (sandalwood, rosewood, etc), as well as from tourism, is threatened. In other areas, Girijan and tribal agitation is to prevent private companies commercially exploiting the habitat of these local peoples (e.g. Chipko in the Himalayas, Appiko in the Western Ghats). Rarely is the issue that of a direct clash of interest between people and earth. Only by keeping these two poles of concern together, as against the interests of commerce and of State control, will there be justice for either people or earth.[12] Economy and ecology are inextricable.

Linkage of Local and Global Perspectives

5. Finally, we need a creative linkage of *local and global* perspectives. These two poles of concern in the inter-connecting web of which we are part can only be very inadequately touched on, for their importance is matched only by their complexity. As we rapidly move towards 2020, the issues between these two polarised worldviews become more crucial for the world's future. In India, for example, while in the 1990s opposition to so many aspects of globalisation was rife – public demonstrations against McDonald's for instance – now the apparent economic benefits are warmly embraced. At the same time, in some ways communalist tensions increase – as is true in many parts of the globe. Other anomalies accompanying the globalising process are all too obvious. Much of the internal strife in Europe, America, Asia bears witness to this.

On this issue, many of us find clarity problematic, and radical social critics in India will see my position as hopelessly compromised. For I still do believe in the gospel of One World – even if an earlier naivete has had to be drastically rethought. However great the need for focus on re-establishing local community life, with the empowerment of local people as a move towards their control of and responsibility for both their economic and their ecologic life, we are still to perceive ourselves as *globally interdependent*. Cultural indigeneity is essential to our being as humans, especially at a time when we see that indigeneity being daily eroded by the modernising process. Yet, our identity and our consciousness as part of the whole human race must mean that at crucial points we are trans-national, pan-tribal, humanly and cosmically inclusive; we need a radically globalised way of perceiving and planning.

Having said that, anyone concerned for global justice is bound to recognise that many aspects of present day market-driven globalisation – political, economic, cultural – are disastrous for the life of local communities in the 'developing world'. Often globalisation is in reality a new form of colonialism, culturally and economically an even more effective take-over than the direct militarism of imperialist expansions in previous centuries. Now the very being of 'third-world' peoples is re-defined in the image of the capitalist culture of the North. Even the policies of macro-aid funding bodies have so often had disastrous effects both on local ecologies and economies. Globalisation is hurting at many local points, such as those weavers and small farmers in Andhra and elsewhere who have been driven to suicide largely because of global pressures on their economies.[13]

Equally, however, it would surely be a retrograde step to attempt a complete reversal of the move towards a more inclusive human consciousness. The new sense of belonging to one human community, is qualitatively different in its potential from all previous imperial and imposed universalism, such as the Pax Romana, or the British Commonwealth.

The opposite of this humane, genuinely participant globalisation is the ethnic intolerance, the tribal belligerence and genocide earlier seen in Biafra and Bosnia, Northern Ireland, Sri-Lanka and Ruanda, and still rampant in parts of the globe – even if both intensified and further complicated by 'religious' commitments. In all these instances, of course, the legacy of colonialisation, outside political or economic pressure, the 'need' for the raw materials or fuel located in the lands of other people, international arms dealing – have been as much the cause as have local tribalisms. But tribal aggression has a very long and very bloody history, whether in Europe, or Africa, or Asia. Nor does the evil side of modern commercial globalisation rule out the potential for great enrichment of human life through cross-cultural interaction. Ecologically, in any case, we are all today bound up together in a single interconnected eco-community, as the now inescapable result of modernisation.

Conclusion: Liturgical Eco-Theology

By way of conclusion, then, for a persuasive eco-faith to emerge, *theological reflection* needs to be as wide-ranging as the concerns of ecology. But, in the life of a faith-community such the Christian church, there are a number of crucial focal-points at which ecclesial ministry can have maximum effect. I shall refer to only one aspect of regular ecclesial life – our worship-forms, our Liturgy. In corporate worship we focus most intently – unless our liturgical life is moribund and meaningless – on the central imagery, the binding themes of faith. By repeated sharing in this corporate matrix of our Christian being, we internalise our faith as a community.

One of the key faith-themes of the 'Alternative Church of South India liturgy,'[14] authorised by the Synod in 1985 (key parts of which are used regularly in such centres as St Mark's, Bangalore, though not widely elsewhere) was precisely this concern for God's creation, incorporated expressly into the Affirmation of Faith, the Offering Prayers, and even into the central prayers at the Lord's Table. In all cases the eco-concern of these prayers is linked closely with our faith-commitment to justice for the oppressed and to peace for the whole world.

In the offering, for example, we pray:

> Glory to God, who has made covenant with all creatures
> ... and entrusted earth and her life to our care...
> We offer the work we do among and with our fellow humans,
> asking you to lead us into your ways of justice and peace.

As we care for this world you have given us,
may we be filled with compassion for all creatures...
Glory to God our sustainer, who loves and cares for all...

Then, in the 'Bread Prayer:'

As this bread is broken and this wine poured out,
Seeker and Saviour of the lost,
we remember again the poor and oppressed of the earth.
As this bread was once scattered seed, O Bread of Life,
sown in the earth to die and rise to new life,
so gather all peoples together in the one humanity of your coming new age.
Restore the broken life of your creation;
heal the disfigured body of your world;
draw all creatures into yourself...

Here is a focal point for faith that, shared in imaginatively, can contribute to the creation of the new eco-vision, the changed perception of our 'home' that is the great need of our time.

Endnotes

1. Further discussion of this theme is found in my Justice Vasudevamurthy Memorial Lecture 1985: *Indian Culture and Earth Care: Facing Our Ecological Crisis.*
2. *Bangalore Theological Forum*, Oct-Dec 1986, p. 150.
3. Cf. e.g. M. Gadgil and R. Guha, *This Fissured Land: An Ecological History of India,* Oxford 1991; also, *Ecology and Equity: The Use and Abuse of Nature in Contemporary India*, London, Routledge 1996. Two other very different but significant publications are: R. Kothari, *Growing Amnesia: An Essay on Poverty and the Human Consciousness*, Viking, New Delhi 1993; Vandana Shiva, *Staying Alive: Women, Ecology and Survival in India*, London 1989.
4. K.C.Abraham, in *Eco-Theology: Voices from South and North*, edited by David C. Hallman, New York, Orbis 1994, p. 65.
5. See, for example, the volumes edited by Anil Agarwal, *The State of India's Environment: Citizens' Report*, New Delhi 1980, 1985, etc.
6. Genesis 1, repeated at each stage of creation.
7. Cf. my *Vision, Tradition, Interpretation*, Berlin, Mouton/De Gruyter 1988, especially chapters 3 and 4.

8 Jyoti Sahi's 1995 Teape Lectures at Cambridge dealt with these themes. Among his writings are his earlier *The Child and the Serpent*, Routledge, London 1984, and an autobiography, *Stepping Stones*, ATC, Bangalore 1985.

9 I discuss this tradition in more detail in, e.g. *Vedantic Approaches to God*, London, Macmillan 1978.

10 Catholic theology in India, until quite recently, far too uncritically assumed the `superiority' of Śaṅkara's Advaitic system within Vedānta and, in general accepted rather uncritically the ontological framework of Advaita within which to develop an Indian Christian theology.

11 A few earlier examples are: S. McFague, *The Body of God: An Ecological Theology*, SCM London 1993; R. R. Ruether, *Gaia and God: An Eco-Feminist Theology of Earth Healing*, Harper, San Francisco 1992; G. Dietrich, *Women's Movements in India: Conceptual and Religious Reflections, Breakthrough*, Bangalore 1988 (There are also more recent such publications).

12 Few Dalit theologians and theoreticians, however, have seen the eco-movement as significant for Dalits. The editor of *Dalit Voice* put this very sharply: 'Environment, nature, ecology have become yet another latest stunt of the upper caste to fool our people' (*Dalit Voice*, April 1991, pp. 4-5). A.P. Nirmal seems to be the only Dalit theologian who, before his untimely death in 1995, came to see the significance of ecology for the emergence of a Dalit identity and the articulation of Dalit consciousness. Cf. his 'Ecology, Ecumenics and Economy in Relation: A New Theological Paradigm', in *Ecology and Development: Theological Perspectives*, Madras, Gurukul 1991.

13 Recounted by M. P. Joseph in a Research Seminar Paper presented at UTC in November 1995.

14 See my article in a Festschrift to Bishop Sundar Clarke, 'Faith and Culture in Interaction: The Alternative CSI Liturgy', in *Reflections*, Madras 1989.

9

'All Loves Excelling': Dialogue on *Bhakti*

Religion in India can be quite bewildering to the stranger. 'Hindu faith' takes many different forms: so many shrines and temples, so many sacred pools and places of pilgrimage, so many rituals and festivals, so many animals, birds, men and women who are said to bear sacred power, so many belief-systems and philosophies, so many scriptures and religious songs, so many esoteric spiritualities, systems of Yoga and astrologies, so many different ways of naming God. It is as if every possible space is filled with some special way of being religious; faith finds such contrasting forms.

Faced with this plethora of possibilities, then, where is an outsider – 'Christian' or any other – to begin in looking at and responding to 'Hindu faith'? My starting point is a Hindu term that would have been greatly treasured by my spiritual forebears, the Wesleys, had they been in touch with Indian spirituality. *Bhakti* is the word I refer to. Its most simple religious meaning is any form of loving devotion, especially religious devotion. Its root (*bhaj*) refers to the 'sharing' of food, or even passionate sharing in sex. And so *bhakti* has come to mean not just 'devotion', but even a sharing passionately in God's love and being consumed by love for God, as the highest goal of the human journey.

'Love divine, all loves excelling' – the first line of a well-known Charles Wesley hymn - was the focus of so many of the Wesleys' hymns. With such an emphasis, rather than ecclesiatical rectitude or even strictly correct doctrine, it is no wonder that the Wesleys, John in particular, were willing to hold out 'a hand of friendship' to any who loved God. In both the British and American contexts a disproportionate number of those prominent in inter-faith affairs have come, like myself, from a Methodist background: Kenneth Cracknell, Wesley Arairajah, Martin Forward, Frank Whaling, David Scott, Diana Eck, Roy Pape, John Cobb, Larry Shinn, R. Blake Michael, Elizabeth Harris, to name just a few from my own generation.

Importance of India's *Bhakti* Movements

This *bhakti*-experience is so significant within Indian religious history that the frequent references in these essays to that form of religious experience is thoroughly justified. Perhaps taking such 'Love divine' as the starting point for understanding Hindu faith betrays my own Methodist bias. Even so, no faithful account of Hindu religious history and its wide range of spiritualities can fail to recognise the crucial importance of this wide-ranging religious phenomenon.

Beginning two or three centuries before Jesus, and still there in the 17th century, wave after wave of what are called the *bhakti* movements swept through different regions and were expressed in the different languages of India. There is much in these movements that *challenged and still challenges* the foundations of some traditional forms of religion. Even if they did not eliminate, they tended to counter a social hierarchy based on a system of purity and pollution; they countered an elitist ritualism based on priestly power and esoteric knowledge. These *bhakti*-movements expressed a much more broadly based *people's indigenous* religiosity.

In turn, such movements inevitably made an impact upon at least some streams within the priestly Brahmanic community.

I recall an occasion when I was sharing in a festival at a nearby Śrī-Vaiṣṇava Kṛṣṇa temple in Bangalore. The previous day I had been asked to give a lecture on the great teacher in their tradition, Rāmānuja. I imagine in that particular temple a good proportion of the great crowd gathered there were Brahmins; others were from so-called 'lower' caste communities. When I turned up the next day it was worship time; the images had been ministered to and taken in procession; the Sanskrit mantras from the ancient scriptures were being chanted by the celebrant priests.

Then, as libation was poured on to the sacred fire and the flames surged up, there was a switch to singing together the Tamil songs of one of their beloved Āḻvār-poets. The 'Āḻvārs' were those 'drowned' in divine love, overflowing with their ecstatic songs to the Lord. Even though the song they were singing was by one who was far from being a Brahmin, immediately there was a dramatic change of mood. Whereas up till then most people were only half-watching the priestly action, perhaps even chatting together, suddenly there was totally attentive devotion as everyone began to sing the songs of intense love for God they had probably learnt as children. They were songs that clearly came from their heart.

(A recent study of *Bhakti* by Israel Selvanayagam, *Kristu Bhakti and Krishna Bhakti: A Christian-Hindu Dialogue Contributing to Comparative Theology,* Christian World Imprints, Delhi 2017, is a valuable aid to understanding in this field).

Bhakti as Intensely Personal

Let me now describe in a little more detail a few of the more significant features of this *bhakti*-religion. In the first place, the focus of these vernacular songs of love is *an intense experience of a God who is eminently personal, and upon whom they felt utterly dependent*. They may recognise other divine figures, known by many names; but for these love-drowned singers, their particular and clearly named Beloved is the one great God of all, in whom every possible good and great quality is found. In these *bhakti* movements, Viṣṇu (especially as embodied either in Kṛṣṇa or in Rāma) and Śiva were the special objects of this devotion.

Of these numerous itinerant poets, passionately singing the praises of their God, quite a few in turn themselves became venerated for their ecstatic devotion. The Tamil Viṣṇu-poet, Nammāḻvār, '*Our* love-drowned one', around the 9th century, was perhaps the greatest of these love-possessed singers. Here are a few typical lines (taken from his 1000 stanza *Tiruvāimoḻi* V.7. And I confess with shame that here I am dependent on English translations, as Tamil is not one of the South Indian languages I became familiar with).

> O Lord of celestial powers,
> In your grace you entered even my heart.
> O Lord of eternal glory, the living Spring of all that lives,
> Father, mother, swallower of the seven worlds...
> You have given me your feet as my sole refuge and path.
> I have nothing to give in return; my soul too is yours...
> You made a person of this worthless self,
> and took me into your service.[1]

The great *theologian* of this God-drowned tradition, Rāmānuja, two centuries or so later, is far more prosaic in style, but still describes a similar vision of God. This *Paramātmā*, or 'Great/Highest Self' is characterised by 'myriads of immeasurable and glorious perfections: he is all-knowing, all-powerful, sovereign over all, none are his equal, none surpass him, his will is always realised, his being is all-illumining, he is wholly free from evil...'. He also lists God's 'lordship, profundity, generosity and compassion', and speaks of God as 'an ocean full of forgiving love for those who take refuge in him, the supremely merciful.'[2]

Theirs, then, was an *intensely personal* experience of God. In the poems, even if not always so clearly in later theology, a feeling of closeness with God is often linked with a strong sense of personal unworthiness, so that the contrast is drawn between our pathetic condition and God's wondrous character – his purity and *beauty* as well as the creative greatness and power to liberate.

God's Beauty and Divine Dance

In fact, there is frequent *aesthetic* emphasis in Hindu spirituality and theology: God is the 'Beautiful One', even seductively attractive, especially in the case of Krishna with his flute-playing. As the Āḻvārs imagine themselves in the role of the cow-girl lovers of Krishna, dancing with him, they often express their passion in erotic terms, well beyond what we find in the biblical Song of Songs.[3] Śiva too is 'the Beautiful One', especially in his wonderful dancing as Naṭarāj, the 'King of Dance.'[4] But, in relation to both, what is to be experienced by the devotee is *the dance of the Lord within their hearts*, in Śiva's case burning up all desire that is not God-directed, and filling their hearts with his dancing bliss.

The divine dance is also *cosmic* in its range. The very name 'Viṣṇu' means 'the pervasive one'. Again and again in the poems God is described as the 'One who wonderfully pervades all things'. I quote again from Tiruvāimoḻi:

> All living beings, all the worlds,
> He holds them all within himself with ease...
> He mingled and merged himself into this universe (II.2:6, 9)

Later[5] the poet becomes a love-sick girl; she feels Kṛṣṇa has left her, yet she feels poignantly aware of his presence at every point where Nature touches her. The imagery is charged with sensuality: she 'caresses the earth', 'points to the red sun' and the 'radiant moon', 'feels the cool wind', 'smells the Tulasi flowers', 'wonders at a standing mountain', is drenched by the pouring rain, 'hugs a tender calf', 'watches the arising of darkly heavy clouds' – and each part of Nature, sensually experienced, brings her parted Lover vividly to mind. And so she calls him back to her heart: 'Come, my Lord'. The sense of God's all-pervasiveness in itself, in other words, did not satisfy her heart.

Tradition Ridiculed, yet Crucial

On occasion too, in various strands of *bhakti* poetry, the need for experience of God in the heart leads to a *ridiculing of ritual tradition*. Tukaram, the 16th century Kṛṣṇa-poet from further north in Maratha, typically writes of the tradition of making pilgrimage to sacred places:

> They bathe in many a sacred river;
> Still their hearts are dry as ever.[6]

This should not, however, be taken as an across-the-board rejection of sacred tradition, with its temples, pilgrimages, sacred places. For the vision of God of nearly all these *bhakti*-saints is grounded in their experience of *special places of pilgrimage and the sacred image* found there. Almost every stanza, too, is filled with allusions to the countless mythic stories through which the various exploits of their God is described. There is a very clear sacred structuring underlying their ecstasy. Yet, it is the *spirit* with which tradition is shared in that counts for them. As the *bhakti*-poet Appar puts it:

> Why bathe in Ganga's stream, or Kaveri?....
> Why chant the Vedas?....
> Why fast and starve, why suffer pains austere?....
> Release is theirs, and theirs alone, who call
> At every time upon the Lord of all.[7]

Guru and Divine Names

And there are many other ways in which this love-centred religion remained plugged into what might be called the power-points of wider Hindu tradition. The *Guru,* or sacred teacher, is one such. Sometimes it is God who is the Guru; at other times an earthly Guru is seen as an embodiment of God. 'Remover of darkness' is what is usually understood as the meaning of the term 'Guru'. Once a disciple accepts that a certain Guru is endowed with special insight, and has the power to guide to the feet of God, then that disciple is expected to submit to the Guru as though to God. So the Guru becomes an essential mediator of divine grace as well as of spiritual wisdom.

One of the ways the Guru guides the disciple is by initiating him/her into a series of secret *Mantras,* or sacred sayings. These will usually include the sacred *Name*: the special Names of God are believed to convey divine power. Reciting them, perhaps the same name over and over again ('Rāma, Rāma, Rāma......'), or maybe the 1000 sacred Names by which the concerned deity's great exploits are summed up, is taken as a sure way to be caught up in the spirit and grace of that holy one. In a number of *bhakti*-groups, praise-songs, or *bhajans*, centred on these Names, are sung corporately by a group of devotees, perhaps throughout the night as a vigil discipline.

So, then, even though some gripped by divine *bhakti* may frequently have been critical of traditional ways of being religious, there are still many ways in which this religion of divine love was plugged into the traditional power-points.

The Contrasting Emotions of *Bhakti*

Again we need to recognise the great range of *contrasting emotion* expressed in many of these *bhakti* songs. On the one hand we see their *ecstasy*, resulting from an overwhelming sense of being loved by God. Because of this the *bhaktas* sometimes laugh and dance and sing with wild abandon. But they also know the *agony*, the sense of loss of that other blissful state, a disconsolate sense of separation from that loving presence. And it is God who is often blamed, as an infatuated lover would her beloved, for having deceived her and left her alone, even though only for a time. In their tears and sighs they may speak of being gripped by a kind of *madness*, the madness of love. And this love-mad state is held up almost as essential if anyone would be a true devotee.

Another contrast appears in descriptions of the *mystery* of the being and character of God. Throughout the poetry and theology of the devotees of Viṣṇu there is a juxtaposing of the otherness and the accessibility of God. It is a 'God-far, God-near' theology.[8]

God's Embodiment on Earth

The nearness of God is often linked with his accessibility both through his *embodiments* on earth and in the sacred images. For, although no Hindu would see God's earthly presence as limited to any image, when the image is consecrated it is then experienced as a transformed embodiment of the divine presence. It too may be called an *avatāra*, just as are God's 'descents' to earth in the form of Rāma, Kṛṣṇa and the other Avatārs. As we noted in the essay above on Avatāra, a Vaiṣṇava theologian of the 13th century (Pillai Lokacharya) speaks with great wonder of the gracious condescension of this God who has put himself, in his image-forms, in the hands of his loved ones, even made himself dependent on their loving ministrations. And theologians like Rāmānuja saw the primary reason for God's 'Descents' as the desire to be near and accessible to those who love him. And yet they are sure that God remains, in his essential being, beyond and unchanged by all the changes and evil and pain of our world. (In view of material covered in previous essays, a substantial portion of the original essay is omitted here and in the following section. For a more detailed look at key issues in Hindu theological discussion, see my *Vedantic Approaches to God*, Macmillan, London 1980).

Śiva as Sacred Focus too

Followers of the 'Great God' Śiva, unlike Viṣṇu-devotees, had no place for the idea of Avatāric embodiments of God. Fitting his image as the Dancer in the fiery cremation grounds and sometimes on the mountains, perhaps dancing wildly with Pārvatī, Śiva is often depicted as more 'other', less subject to any control. That, though, is but one of the many and contrasting pictures we are given of Śiva. No God has ever encompassed such paradoxical pictures. He is both a wandering ascetic and a phallic God of incredible erotic feats. He is both the Destroyer and the Healer. He dances his fiercely destructive Tāṇḍava, and his tranquil peace-bestowing Lāsya dances. He is adorned with a necklace of skulls; yet he also bears in his throat the poison drunk in order to save his loved ones. Hence his name, 'He with the blue-black throat'.

The Śiva of some of the sacred stories can inspire awe and fear and even seemingly deliberate disgust; yet he also evokes the most wonderful emotions of love and rapture. Here are two stanzas from an early Śiva-lover Tirunāvukkarasar (Appar) Swami;:[9]

> Thou to me art parents, Lord
> All the family, friends I need;

Thou to me art loved ones fair
Thou art treasure rich indeed....

As the vina's pure sound, as the moonlight at even,
As the south wind's soft breath, as the spring's growing heat,
As the pool hovered over by whispering bees,
So sweet is the shade of our Father-Lord's feet.

Contrast with Ritualism

We should, too, note an important difference between the attitude found in *bhakti*-religion based on God-love and that of a number of other religious attitudes within the Hindu traditions. For these God-lovers the Focus of their devotion is never a means to some other end; the love-experience of God is an *end in itself.* In other words, loving relationship with God is the ultimate Goal of our existence.

This contrasts, for example, with that classical Ritualism (Pūrva-mīmāṃsa) that emerged within Indian tradition which developed a philosophy of religion based on the principle that the priestly ritual is in itself an ultimate value. Of itself it will ensure the well-being of the doer, whatever blessing it is the ritual-doer desires. The *attitude* with which religious action is done matters little; the ritual doing is all. And the concerned god is merely an incidental participant in the process. There must be very few such ideological ritualists in India today; but that kind of magical faith in the efficacy of certain repeated actions, especially when one's tradition says its ritual is efficacious, is found in many cultures and religious traditions.

Classical Yoga in many ways is thoroughly dissimilar to ritualism. Yet, in one regard there is a strange similarity in the techniques of one form of classical Yoga. God is included as a necessary focus for meditation – necessary in that the Lord encapsulates those higher qualities of freedom, knowledge, tranquillity that the soul desires. Gradually, as this higher state of existence is realised, there is the attaining of self-isolation, or selfhood alone (*ātma-kaivalya*), and God as a distinct being fades from view. To the true God-lover, however, that Beloved can never fade from view; while God may be seen as the means to blessing, more importantly he becomes the great Goal of life, the *summum bonum*.

A Religion of Grace

Bhakti-religion, as we have already seen to some extent, was a religion of *grace*. There was the experience of God's compassion, acceptance, forgiveness and the possibility of new life, even for those who saw themselves as miserable sinners. A few lines again from Nammāḻvār:

> I have become his true lover; and he is mine.
> So strong the sin; but when his grace comes, it shall come...
> Like a ship caught in stormy seas crying out in distress,
> I stood trembling in the ocean of birth and called.
> With exceeding grace, divine symbols in hand,
> He heard, he came, and became one with me....
> Of his own sweet grace he became one with me.[10]

A few centuries later there was a serious division within this particular community – mainly concerning how divine grace is to be understood (Discussed at length in essay five above). There were those who taught the *cat-way* and those who taught the *monkey-way*. The young cat is taken up helpless by its mother; the young monkey has to cling to its mother. The debate, in other words, is very close to that of Pelagius and Augustine within Christian theology. Is divine grace utterly predetermined and independent, taking up the helpless sinner regardless of that person's own struggle? Or, does divine grace require some degree of cooperation from the sinner? There were in fact 17 other key points of disagreement between these two branches of Sri-Vaishnavism. The sovereignty of grace, though, was at the centre of their debate.

Role of Karma?

Closely linked to the experience of divine grace is a doctrine that formed the background to almost all the great religious traditions of India – Jaina, Buddhist, Hindu, Sikh – and became deeply ingrained in the common Indian worldview. I refer to the ancient notion of *karma.* Literally the term means `action', referring to all those actions done in the past – not merely in this life, but in that endless series of births and rebirths through which the soul's eternal journey is made. Each action – rather like seed sown – at some point has to `bear its fruit', or we might say `reap its harvest', for good or for ill. It is the power of this karmic process that keeps the soul bound to the cycle of birth and rebirth. The particular body given to a soul – as animal, demon, outcaste, woman, Brahmin, heavenly nymph – as well as the degree of pain or pleasure experienced in that life, is determined by past *karma.*

We should not over-emphasise Hindu belief in this doctrine. For, there is evidence that for many 'Hindus' today (especially the more urbanised) it is not an essential part of their worldview. Rural people, though, when going through a period of tragedy, may often be heard to cry out: `What great sin did I commit that this should be my *karma*?' In theory, of course, it also works the other way – and this is what the modern Hindu apologist will emphasise: `What I do now will determine what I will yet become'. And these individual soul-cycles are part of a broader cosmic cycle of the withdrawing and the recreation of the whole universe again and again.

The great quest, then, has been for some permanent liberation (*mukti, moksha*) from this karmic bondage. `Who will set me free from this body of death?': Paul's soulful cry, is slightly extended – `Who will set me free from this body of death – and from rebirth?' We do find references from time to time, in the love-songs of *bhaktas*, to the need for release from karmic bondage. Usually this will be by way of joyful celebration that divine grace has broken the chain. The `ocean of birth' of which Nammāḻvār wrote (above), into which the Lord came and from which the trembling sinner was saved, is this karmic cycle.

For all God's creatures, though, this karmic law of cause-effect is all-pervading, part and parcel of the creative process. And the love-singers are quite clear that it is *God* who has caused and who controls this cycle of bondage.

> I have reached you, yet not attained you;
> Between us you have placed this body;
> Tied me tightly to it with strong cords of karma,
> Covered the wound neatly,
> and cast me out into this deceptive world.[10]

The question is then: does God, `overwhelmed by a compassion that is unable to bear the suffering of his creatures' (to quote a *bhakti*-theologian, Rāmānuja), intervene in the process of moral cause and effect that he himself as Creator has initiated? Does God break that binding chain forged as part of his creation's working, in order to set his loved ones free? And this raises the question, if in different terms, both of Law's relation to Grace (as in Christian theology) and, less directly, the mystery of divine love and creaturely suffering that religious thinkers have always and everywhere found so problematic. Certainly for those Hindu people of faith who put God's love at the centre, the main sentiment they express is a joyful confidence that God has and will set them free. *Karma*, or the action-reaction process, is sidelined. Indeed, most of the time they seem to have forgotten altogether about that fatal and eternal bondage, so caught up are they by divine Love.

The Meaning of *Dharma*?

Whatever may have been their experience at a personal level, no serious discussion of Hindu faith can escape a hard look at the *social outworking* of the doctrine of *karma* and thus its correlate *dharma*. So far I have deliberately focussed primarily on `Hindu *faith*' in this essay, rather than on a more general consideration of Hindu cultural values and social life. These are, however, very closely interwoven into Hindu tradition, a point which Hindu apologists themselves often make quite proudly. Not for them, they assert, the western dichotomy of religion, as personal conviction, and culture, as social life. *Dharma*, meaning the right ordering of things, has personal, social, and cosmic dimensions; it is built into the intrinsic structuring of every aspect of our existence.

The problem is, no talk of *dharma* can avoid the issue of *caste*. It is often said that caste, historically, is not a tradition based on 'religion'. As a social arrangement, it has been merely a division of functions within society: some were best equipped to be priests, scholars, meditators; others to rule and defend the State; others to do business; others to be artisans and manual workers.

It is also said this was once a *flexible* social arrangement; individuals and even whole communities moved freely from one caste identity to another. And there is indeed evidence of mobility in the period before '*dharma*' became as rigidly stratified as in recent centuries. At least the Law in India today is clear that there must be no discrimination on the basis of caste, and certainly no practice of untouchability. Moreover, during the past two centuries there have been good numbers of social reformers, often practising Hindus and sometimes their religious leaders, who have worked for radical change of attitude.

Unfortunately, whether based on social custom or religious sanction, in some areas discrimination is still strong, even some temples refusing admission to 'non-Hindus'. A few years ago, much to the embarrassment of the Brahmin friend accompanying me, though dressed appropriately, and having received *darśan* from and talked with the Swamiji for 30 minutes, I was barred from entering beyond the outer court of Rāmānuja's great temple at Sri Rangam in Tamilnadu. In recent years considerable progress has been made in admitting 'Dalit' people into temples; yet, in some regions, especially as Dalit consciousness strengthens, there is evidence of hardening of ancient prejudice, and social identities become more restrictive.

Whatever can be said by way of critical analysis of the caste system and its role within Hindu *dharma*, here let me hasten to admit as someone from Britain, that in the history of my own country, and within the 'Christian' tradition generally, there have also been deeply divisive social structures and attitudes undergirding them that have been disgracefully discriminating. Honesty and self-criticism is called for here. We all frequently fail to embody within our life in the world some of the key principles in our faith.

Summary of Key Social Features of the 'Love-drowned'

What, though, has been the case when Hindu people have been 'drowned' in the experience of divine love? Surely this inwardly transforming experience at least has the *potential* for a dynamic re-viewing and re-shaping of human community. And the *bhakti*-movements have clearly resulted in some forms of social change. For wider transformation to take place, however, there has to be an undergirding worldview that will move the experience of inner liberation on from personal to corporate vision, a worldview in which social transformation is intrinsic. What can we see in the *bhakti* worldview that potentially at least would have made an impact upon the wider life of the community?

1. *Potential for Social Openness*

In the first place there is evidence of *social openness* in these movements. For it was a deeply held conviction that divine grace is open to all who have true faith in God, and this in spite of the sacral ordering of society in which by tradition some were born as the elite pure, and others in a hierarchy of less privileged, increasingly less pure, communities of people.

In other words there is something fundamental to this *bhakti* experience that runs counter to elements within dharmic tradition. Large numbers of those caught up in *bhakti*-movements, even those who came to be venerated almost as divine figures (their images are found in Vaiṣṇava temples), were from the so-called lower castes; a few too were women. There were also such anomalous instances to be found in Vedic and Puranic sources. In any case, within the later *bhakti*-movements, should we not expect a sense of dissatisfaction with the way things are socially? For *bhakti* preachers, however, the priority was the transforming inner experience of God's wonderful love. Few voiced dissatisfaction in terms aimed directly at change in community.

The 'Gospel of Hinduism' (the Gītā) in what is called its 'final word' (18.66) seems clearly to make the inherited requirements of *dharma* quite relative in comparison with the wonder of divine grace and love:

> Give up all your *dharmas*, take me alone as your refuge,
> I will set you free from all your sins, have no fear...
> This is my highest secret that I tell you,
> I love you well...

And yet, the status quo of *dharma* has, through the ages, remained largely intact. The parallels within evangelical Christianity (in 19th century Britain for example) are obvious, even though there are those who see a direct link between the equality found in evangelical Christian faith and the 19th century socialist movement. We might note that the leaders of the very first Trade Union formed in Britain – the Tolpuddle Martyrs, farmworkers in Dorset – were Methodist preachers.

So was it the case, as Indian Marxist historians like D. D. Kosambi argued, that all *bhakti*-religion was Brahmanic manipulation by which the lower orders were lulled into being unconcerned about the take-over of their lands and their culture by Brahmin-dominated colonialists? Perhaps this is one element in the process. But it is far from all that can be seen in the *bhakti* movements, any more than the Methodist movement in 18th century Britain was primarily a way by which the Establishment and pioneering Industrialists were ensuring they could avoid the kind of revolutionary violence that overtook France. Even so, preaching divine grace for all, by Christian or Hindu, in itself clearly does not ensure that wider, more inclusive transformation that is surely God's purpose for his world. The openness of grace requires also a wider world-view, a more inclusive theology that encourages wider transformation.

In passing we should also note that from the beginning within Hindu faith there has been the widespread practice of charitable giving to the needy. Significantly, this has been called 'doing one's *dharma*', the very term I've been translating as 'the proper ordering of things'. As is usually the case with 'charity', it is usually not intended to lead directly to wider social transformation. Alms-giving rarely has this dynamic intent, and may even be intended mainly to acquire merit for the giver. Only rarely would it be seen as an expression of divine love reaching out to all, especially those in need.

Yet, in the past century or two, with the upsurge of reform movements within Hinduism, there are increasing numbers of groups emerging that take belief in the all-embracing compassion of God to mean that all are deserving of such help as can be given. For example, I was once involved in helping the large numbers of people suffering, especially in that area (Godavari Delta region), from the terrible effects of leprosy, working collaboratively with a Hindu group called '*Jīva-Kāruṇya-Sangha*', which literally means the Society for Life-Compassion. Other outstanding examples are the social service of the Ramakrishna Mission, and the remarkable 19th century Swami Narayana movement (especially among the Ezhalavas) in Kerala (who was a devout Advaitin as it happens).

God's 'compassion' for all living creatures is often expressed in the image of Kṛṣṇa holding aloft the top portion of his sacred mountain, providing shelter for cattle and other living things when a great flood threatened them. More frequently, though, 'compassion for all creatures' has been ascribed to the Buddha. And it may be that his influence lies behind the frequent use of this term in that 'Gospel of Hinduism', the Bhagavad Gītā, written not long before the time of Jesus. For, there are several other signs of Buddhist influence in the Gītā.

2. *Community Sharing: Social Change*

Any who describe Hindu religious faith as entirely an individual matter, with no serious social dimension, clearly misinterpret that faith. In any case we have only to look at the immensely important role of their many festivals, with their strongly community character, to know that with Hindu religion 'individualism' is hardly the word that comes to mind.

Probably the most striking instance of a *bhakti*-movement that led to social awareness was that of the *Lingāyats*, devotees of Śiva in Karnataka, S. India, whose great reformer was Basava in the 12th century. This was a movement deeply and frequently critical of all caste distinctions.[11] In fact, in their religious experience rigorously ethical standards – including the duties of hard work, mutual fraternal support, caring for widows, and meeting for regular sharing in their 'Hall of Experience' – were an intrinsic part of faith in God. It is sad that this virile devotional movement has to some extent become yet another caste community fighting for political benefits for itself. The less 'political', more 'community' concern is still there, but we can see that even the deeply experienced sense of God's presence with all manner of people in the end failed to break through the limiting structures of caste.

There is another aspect of at least some *bhakti*-faith that surely should encourage the sense of need for wider social change. This is the conviction that the *new age of God* has now dawned as people everywhere are being touched by God's grace. This kind of 'realised eschatology' can be seen in that recent Hindu movement to which quite large numbers of western young people have been attracted. I refer to the *Hare Kṛṣṇa* movement. This is the nearest Hindu equivalent of charismatic Christianity when it too is also socially aware. But listen again to the words of that love-drowned singer Nammāḻvār from the deep South of India more than 1000 years ago, as he describes (in his *Tiruvāimoḻi* V.1.7, 9-10) what he sees as the inbreaking of a wondrous New Age:

> Rejoice! Rejoice! Rejoice! Gone is life's curse,
> Hell's agony destroyed;
> Death has no place here;
> Even the power of the dark age is eclipsed.
> See for yourself!
>
> Those beloved of our discus-wielding Lord, come to stay,
> Uproot disease, hatred, poverty and pain
> which conquer this earth.
> With melodious songs they leap, they dance in ecstasy,
> and fly all over this earth....[12]

Here, clearly, is another aspect of *bhakti*-faith with the potential for dynamic social transformation.

3. Creation as 'Body of God'

(Much of the following is, in differing ways, found in earlier essays above; the issues are so central that brief repetition is justified). An all-important strand in the worldview of a large section of *bhakti*-people needs to be affirmed and re-affirmed. It was a faith-image beloved by God-lovers, and was to become the interpretive key to the immensely important theological system of Rāmānuja in the 11th century. The whole created world, they affirmed, is *related to God as a body to its inmost self*, by which it is animated, and upon which it is utterly dependent. As early as key Vedic writings perhaps eighteen centuries before Rāmānuja, and in many other scriptures, including the Gītā, Hindu tradition gives prominence to this image of God. You understand nothing about the ways of God, said this *bhakti* theologian, unless you recognise that you and your universe relate to God inseparably as a body to the soul by which it lives.

Here we see another Christian parallel, though, apart from Process Theologians such as Charles Hartshorne, John Cobb and others, in general it is *women* theologians who have seen in the body a way of understanding God's relationship to us. I have so far made no reference to the importance of the feminine at the very heart of God-thinking within Hinduism. In this 'inseparable relationship' between God and the universe, it is the *beloved Lady of the Lord* who is most inextricably 'inseparable'. It is the *Devī*, the feminine deity, who functions as the activating Power of creation, sometimes even the essential Mediatrix of salvation, even though remaining dependent upon the 'Father and Mother of all'. But precise theologising here is difficult. God, certainly Śiva, is often depicted as one in whom both Male and Female are eternally merged. Hence the androgynous icon of Śiva as half-man, half-women.

Now back to the body-talk of *bhakti*. The great significance of this worldview is that *relationship* takes on an ultimate character. In particular God's relationship to us is not an experience that has to be superseded by some further stage of undifferentiated merging. The *bhakti*-theologians were fiercely adamant about this. Eternal love calls for eternal relationship, not for an eternity of merged oneness.

4. Cosmic Realism and Divine Playfulness

And because along with this there is an unrelenting cosmic *realism*, then the whole creative process, with all the changes and distinctions that emerge in that process, at the very least are real. Even when mistaken, our cognitive experiences in the world are real. *Created existence is real, affirms Rāmānuja, because it is the real, effective work of God, the 'Real of reals'* (*satyasya-satya*). The world's dependence on God's animating life and power is ever real. It is only because that power is mysterious and miraculous that in scripture creation is called the '*māyā*' of God. Nor is the realness of things diminished by the idea that God's creating and saving activities are all his '*līlā*', his *playfulness* – often found in *bhakti* writing, along with the image of God as Dancer.

Such an emphasis on playfulness, though, means we need to be very nuanced in our way of thinking about *divine purpose* in Hindu theology. Play doesn't rule out purpose; but it has to be thought of as something more than a so-far-unachieved goal. Then, too, there is the question of how thoroughly God was bound up in the struggles and sufferings of his creation, in the way that at least some Christians are led to believe because of the cross of Jesus. Do the struggles of Rama and Krishna lead to real inner pain and tears? Even so, the claim of the theologians of God-love that all embodiment is materially *real* is still very significant.

5. The Trans-relational View

There are, then, as with most religious traditions, anomalies regarding human community within the attitude of India's God-lovers. Equally and perhaps even more important has been the emerging dominance (for at least a millennium) of an understanding of the intrinsic status of creation and human life, that sees *trans-relational* being alone as ultimately real. Instead of *relationship*, it was unrelated and therefore undifferentiated selfhood, understood as pure *Consciousness*, that became the model for the ultimately real. So, *māyā* became an illusory veil through which all cosmic and human life is to be perceived. When looked at from the perspective of the highest Brahman, all the natural distinctions we experience at our unenlightened state are seen as lacking that reality which is to be experienced by the truly enlightened. It is when we are free from all relationship and the dependencies this entails that we can be ultimately free.

To the God-lovers and their theologians, though, certainly of most Vaiṣṇava traditions, it was anathema to lose sight of that final goal of *inseparable fellowship with God and absolute dependence on God*, an intimacy in which the distinctiveness of each soul too is never lost, even in the fellowship of heaven.

I trust that it is very clear how much there is in Hindu *bhakti*-faith and its undergirding theological insights that can challenge us. There are clearly a number of aspects of Hindu faith by which our own faith as Christians can be enriched. And such enrichment is not merely by way of esoteric spiritual disciplines that can 'expand our inner consciousness', as many in the West tend to see the value of 'Eastern religious experience'. Nor is it only by way of cultural values that can counter western aggressiveness, with our destructive relationship to nature. There can also be an enabling of a deeper sense of the wonder that is God, the wonder of God's all-embracing love and all-pervading, all-embodying presence. Within *bhakti*-religion, too, we see exuberant, even transporting expressions of faith in what Charles Wesley described as 'Love divine, all loves excelling'. Let those of us who are Jesus-followers go on looking at and engaging at depth with Hindu faith, not with the aim of undermining that faith, but that we may be the more faithful to the God and Father of our Lord Jesus Christ at the centre of our own faith.

Endnotes

1. From his 1000-stanza 'Tiruvaimoḻi' V.7.7; translation by S. Bharati and S. Lakshmi, *The Tiruvaimoli of Nammalvar,* Melkote, 1987.
2. *Śrī-Bhāṣya* IV.4.22. For further on theology of Rāmānuja see John Carman, *The Theology of Rāmānuja,* New Haven, Yale, 1974; Julius Lipner, *The Face of Truth,* London, Macmillan, 1986.

3. For a detailed account of the God-lovers' contrasting emotions see F. Hardy, *Viraha Bhakti: The Early Hisory of Krishna Bhakti in South India,* Delhi: Oxford, 1983.
4. See I.V. Peterson, *Poems to Śiva: The Hymns of the Tamil Saints*, Motilal Banarsidass, Delhi, 1991, pp. 286-92.
5. Hardy, *op.cit. passim;* See also Glenn Yocum, *Hymns to the Dancing Siva,* New Delhi: Heritage, 1982.
6. See Peterson, *op.cit.*, 261-62.
7. See Yocum, *op.cit.*, 181.
8. (With R.D. Kaylor as co-author) *God Far, God Near: An Interpretation of the thought of Nammalvar*, Bombay 1981. An important contribution to this issue is John Carman's *Majesty and Meekness: A Comparative Study in the Concept of God,* Grand Rapids, Eerdmans, 1994.
9. Adapted from the translation of F. Kingsbury and G.E. Phillips, *Hymns of the Tamil Saivite Saints,* OUP: Calcutta and London, 1921, p. 4.
10. Adapted from Methodist Missionary J.S. M. Hooper's translation in *Hymns of the Āḻvārs,* Association Press: Calcutta, 1929.
11. See e.g. A.K. Ramanujan, *Speaking of Śiva,* Penguin Books: Middlesex, 1973.
12. Bharati and Lakshmi's translation.

Concluding Comments
Swimming Against Strong Currents?

In these essays as a whole, it can be seen that the theological position I argue for swims against some strong contemporary currents.

1. Serious discussion of the issues debated historically among Vedāntins with differing views has generally not been found among those teaching Hindu religious thought in recent years, especially for anyone eager to understand the theological implications of those Vedāntic views. Rather, the form of Advaita propounded by *Śañkara* is usually assumed to be both intellectually and spiritually superior, as well as being a more viable account of Vedāntic tradition. This was certainly the view of those western scholars introducing Indian thought to a wider readership in the 19th century. Even S. Radhakrishnan, who clearly favoured Śañkara's interpretation, criticised those who failed to recognise at least the existence of Vedāntic theism, and 'persist in foisting on Hinduism as a whole the theory of abstract monism' (*Indian Philosophy*, 2 vols. 1930, 2nd edit. p.712). In general – and this was so with Radhakrishnan too - 'authentic' Advaita Vedānta is seen as 'philosophical' in form, even 'pure philosophy', while Rāmānuja's position is dismissed as 'theology', and therefore mere 'dogma'. Enough has been said on this issue in the preceding essays.

On the other hand an approach by a western scholar, such as C.J. Bartley recently, who with outstanding precision (in *The Theology of Ramanuja: Realism and Religion,* Routledge 2016) makes clear the metaphysical and epistemological skill of Rāmānuja, does not allow sufficient weight to the devotional *passion* to be seen at crucial points in his writings. The words 'Thelogy' and 'Religion' in Bartley's title are rather misleading: there is a great deal of *logic*, skilfully argued and copiously referenced, but we see little of the Acharya's intensely religious devotion to *theos*.

2. Then, a very different but marked strand of global thinking in recent decades (including 'alternative' cultural movements) tends to an *interiority* that seeks ultimate meaning within the individual self. Western seekers who look eastwards for a more authentic spirituality have generally been attracted to those gurus whose teaching is more in tune with the non-dualism of Advaita. Great numbers, too, have come to practise Yoga – and often greatly benefitted by this emphasis on turning away from the distracting stimuli of modern life, even if it be but brief oases of mind-calming. While we should remember that Yoga is not necessarily linked to a Śaṅkara-style worldview, the emphasis of Rāmānuja on both the glorious personal qualities of God, and the total reality of the objective world – emphases that I've applauded – seems rarely to appeal to 'the modern mind-set'.

We may note, too, modernity's growing recognition (in works of science-fiction, for example) with what seems like the 'illusoriness' of our world, as science seems more and more to uncover its mysterious nature, its multiple layers of being. At every level of our human life – individual or social, psychological or physical, private or public, religious or secular – things are rarely what they may at first seem to be.

Was Śaṅkara, then, with his appeal to *māyā* and other such ways of drawing attention to the illusory quality of our world, much closer to the truth of things than I allowed in my earlier accounts of India's religious thought? Was his position more metaphysically tenable than that of Rāmānuja?

I have to reply with a 'maybe' and a 'perhaps not'! Yes, there is more to our world than at first appears. The Upanishadic '*neti, neti*' qualification to be added to every statement we make means, as Rāmānuja also accepted, that our verbal statements about God can never be the final word. Religious traditions generally recognise, and usually wonder at, those dimensions of our world's being that are 'beyond understanding'. It is obvious, too, that taking our sacred words as conveying Truth, and Truth that we are expected to have significant grasp of, does not entail taking their meaning literally and unquestioningly (See also Rowan Williams, *The Edge of Words,* 2014, and Frances Young, *Construing the Cross,* 2014). Yet, accepting the 'beyondness' of revelatory Truth does not mean that we need no longer strive for verbal and conceptual clarity. Nor does it mean, in terms of ultimate faith, that *relationship* is to be down-graded (as is found in some Eastern teaching).

There is, too, the Vedāntic teaching about the 'confused identity' (*bhrama*) we too often hold. This is when outer physical being is seen as the essence of things, as our selfhood. In other words, at the heart of Vedānta too there is recognition of great *mystery* in our world's life and our place in it. Even so, with Rāmānuja we still need to affirm the full reality of our world of bodies and physical being, our embodied world, along with its glorious wonders; for it is a God-given creation, and even shares the embodied life of the Creator.

3. In recent decades there has been a growing rejection of 'monotheistic' thinking, of a belief in one divine Being, one Creator, one who in some way is God of all (especially when that Being is portrayed in masculine terms). As an ardent eco-lover I find especially difficult the common assumption that a 'Christian' doctrine of creation *necessarily* down-values the life of creation, exalting human mastery of creation in the destructive way typical of modern existence generally. The penultimate essay above outlines sufficiently my understanding of a pro-creation theology.

There is some irony in the fact that eco-feminist theologians have frequently spoken of creation as the 'body of God'; yet, even in India, very few have been willing to acknowledge the role of this body-image in such a prominent strand of Hindu theology.

4. Also noted in some of the essays above is how *Dalit* Theology, from the 1970s to the 1990s, was unwilling to allow value to the environmentalist movement, or to creation-centred thinking. A number, no doubt, have found problematic the famous Rigvedic passage describing creation as deriving from a divine body, seen in the hierarchical terms of Brāhmins having come from the mouth, Kṣatriyas from the shoulders, Vaiśyas from the thighs, and Śūdras from the feet. In any case, generally speaking, until recently theology of a more 'critical' kind in India has tended to give far greater weight to socio-political theory and economic analysis, rather than to either the idealism of the Greens, or to other religio-cultural commitments seeking to engage in interfaith dialogue – with which some of the essays above may appear to be more in tune.

5. Very different from either of these two positions are those powerful fundamentalist movements in which a given scripture, interpreted literally, is held exclusively to carry absolute authority, and all other sacred traditions are condemned as against the true way, perhaps as 'demonic'. While such extreme 'othering' is not central to either Hindu or Christian communities in India, the dangers are there and appear to be growing. Any forms of 'fundamentalism' make impossible the dialogical relationship aimed for in these essays. At its root 'fundamentalism' is primarily based on a socio-cultural ideology, often linked with forms of 'tribalist' nationalism. Hence we find forms of this phenomenon even in Buddhist and Hindu communities, when ultra-nationalist identities emerge. When religious, social and in the end *human* identities are given such sharp edges that all other human considerations are lost, then creative dialogical engagement, or inclusive human community life, is also lost. Thus, in some Christian communities, for example, 'interfaith' engagement may even be thought of as 'anti-Christ'.

Less extreme conservatives may argue that to allow the theology of one religious tradition to impinge upon another is to lose the 'integrity' of that faith. Such a rigid view of tradition misunderstands both the dynamic character of faith and the interpenetrative nature of the traditions in which they are embedded. For Christians, even a quick look at the New Testament should make this clear! Certainly such 'interpenetration' can be clearly seen in the millennia-long process that shaped the religious life and thought of India.

There are, then, numerous attitudinal currents against which the ideas offered in the above essays have to swim, striking out as best they might. Let us hope they do not all sink beneath the waves! Sink or swim, the centre of my own religious faith – however much enriched by the dialogical engagement described in these essays – that centre remains the Christ who has been the main-spring of my thinking and my essential being for so many decades. Rāmānuja has, I believe, enhanced this process for me, and I am thankful.

Endnote

1. *The Face of Truth: A Study of Meaning and Metaphysics in the Vedāntic Theology of Rāmānuja.* Julius J. Lipner seems to take theology and religious experience more seriously than Bartley.

BIBLIOGRAPHY

Abraham, K.C., 'A Theological Response to the Ecological Crisis' in *Ecotheology: Voices from South and North*, ed. D.G. Hallman (WCC, Geneva, 1994) Jointly published by Orbis, New York, 1994.

Adidevananda, Swami (trans.), *Stotra-ratna of Yamunāchārya* (Madras, 1967).

Agarwal, A. (ed.), *The State of India's Environment: Citizens' Report* (Centre for Science and Environment, New Delhi, 1982 onwards).

Aiyangar, M.B.V. (trans.), Rangacharya M. (trans.), *The Vedanta-sutras, with the Śrī-Bhāṣya of Rāmānujāchārya* (Brahmavadin Press, Madras, 1899).

Aiyengar, C.R. Srinivasa, *The Life and Teachings of Śrī Rāmānujāchārya* (R. Venkateshwar, Madras, 1908).

Annangaracharya, P.B. (ed.), *Śrī Bhagavad Rāmānuja Grantha-māla* (Kanchipuram, 1956).

Ayyangar, M.B. Narasimha, (trans.), *Vedānta-sāra of Rāmānuja* (Adyar, 1953).

Ayyangar, M.R. Rajagopala, (ed. & trans.), *Vedārtha-Saṃgraha of Rāmānujāchārya* (Author, Madras, 1956).

Bailey, G. (ed.), *Hinduism in India, Vol. I*, series ed. G.A. Oddie (Sage Publications, New Delhi, 2017).

Baillie, J., *Our Knowledge of God* (OUP, London, 1939).

Bartley, C.J., *The Theology of Rāmānuja: Realism and Religion* (Routledge, Abingdon, 2016).

Bhashyam, K. (trans.), *Vedānta-dīpa of Rāmānuja* (Ubhaya Vedanta Granthamala, Madras, 1957).

Bhatt, S.R., *Studies in Rāmānuja Vedānta* (Heritage, New Delhi, 1975).

Bhattacharya, A., *Studies in Post-Śañkara Dialectics* (University of Calcutta, Calcutta, 1936).

Buitenen, van J.A.B. (ed. & trans.), *Rāmānuja's Vedārthasamgraha* (Deccan College, Poona (Pune), 1956).

——— (ed. & trans.), *Yāmuna's Āgama-prāmāṇya* (Rāmānuja Research Society, Madras, 1971).

Carman, J.B., *The Theology of Rāmānuja: An Essay in Interreligious Understanding* (Yale University Press, New Haven, 1974).

Clarke, Sathi., *Dalits and Christianity: Subaltern Religion and Liberation Theology in South India* (OUP, Delhi, 1998).

Dietrich, G., *Women's Movements in India: Conceptual and Religious Reflections, Breakthrough* (Breakthrough Publications, Bangalore, 1988).

Dunn, B.P., *A.J. Appasamy and His Reading of Ramanuja: A Comparative Study of Divine Embodiment* (OUP, Oxford, 2016).

Eilberg-Schwartz, H., *Religious Reflections on the Human Body*, ed. J.M. Law (Indiana University Press, Indianapolis, 1995).

Eliade, M., *Images and Symbols: Studies in Religious Symbolism* (Sheed and Ward, New York, 1961).

Forward, M. (ed.), *Ultimate Visions: Reflections of the Religions We Choose* (Oneworld Publications, Oxford, 1995).

Fox, M., *Original Blessing* (Bear and Co., Santa Fe, 1983).

Gadgil, M., *Ecology and Equity: The Use and Abuse of Nature in Contemporary India* (Routledge, London, 1996).

Gadgil, M., Guha, R., *This Fissured Land: An Ecological History of India* (OUP, New Delhi, 1993).

Govindacharya, A., *The Life of Rāmānujāchārya* (S. Murthy, Madras, 1906).

Gupta, S.K. (trans.), *Madhusūdana Sarasvati on the Bhagavad Gītā* (Motilal Banarsidass, Delhi, 1977).

Hohenberger, A. (trans.), *Vedānta-dīpa of Rāmānuja* (University of Bonn, Bonn, 1964).

Hooper, J.S.M., *Hymns of the Āḻvārs* (Association Press, Calcutta, 1929).

Iyengar, M.B. Narasimha, (trans.), *The Tattva-Traya of Lokacharya* (M.C. Krishnan, Madras, 1966).

Kaylor, R.D., Venkatachari, K.K.A., *God-far, God-near: An Interpretation of the Thought of Nammāḻvār* (Ananthacharya Indological Research Institute, Bombay, 1981).

Kingsbury, F., Phillips, G.E., *Hymns of the Tamil Śaivite Saints* (Association Press, Calcutta, 1921).

Kothari, R., *Growing Amnesia: An Essay on Poverty and the Human Consciousness* (Viking, New Delhi, 1993).

Lipner, J.J., *The Face of Truth: A Study of Meaning and Metaphysics in the Vedāntic Theology of Rāmānuja* (Macmillan, London, 1986).

Lott, E.J., *God and the Universe in the Vedāntic Theology of Rāmānuja* (Rāmānuja Research Society, Madras, 1976).

———, 'The Fulness and Freedom of the Supreme Lord: Madhva's Radical Theism' in *Bangalore Theological Forum, Vol. IX, No.2* (UTC, Bangalore, 1977).

———, 'Divine Grace in Indian Religious Systems' in *Brahma Vādin, Vol. 14* (Vivekananda Kendra, Madras, 1979).

———, *Vedantic Approaches to God* (Macmillan, London & New York, 1980).

———, 'Rāmānuja's Śarīra-Śarīrī-Bhāva: A Conceptual Analysis' in *Studies in Rāmānuja* (Rāmānuja Vedānta Centre, Madras, 1980).

———, 'Iconic Vision and Cosmic Viewpoint in Rāmānuja's Vedānta' in *Proceedings of the Seminar on "Temple Art & Architecture" Held in March 1980*, ed. K.K.A. Venkatachari

(Ananthacharya Indological Research Institute, Bombay, 1981).

———, 'Madhva's Theology of Transcendent Grace' in *Divine Grace and Human Response*, ed. C.M. Vadakekara (Asirvanam Benedictine Monastery, Bangalore, 1981).

———, 'The Significance of Rāmānuja Darśana in Vedantic Debate' in *Rāmānuja Vāṇī* (Rāmānuja Research Society, Madras, 1982).

———, 'Evaluating Vedantic Types of Transcendence' in *Rāmānuja Vāṇī* (Rāmānuja Research Society, Madras, 1985).

———, 'The Divine Drum: Interpreting a Primal Symbol' in *Śrī Andal: Her Contribution to Literature, Philosophy, Religion and Art* (Rāmānuja Vedānta Centre, Madras, 1985).

———, *Indian Culture and Earth Care: Facing Our Ecological Crisis* (Indian Institute of World Culture, Bangalore, 1986).

———, 'The Mythic Symbol Avatāra in Indian Conceptual Formulations' in *Dialogue & Alliance, Vol. I* (International Religious Foundation, New York, 1987).

———, *Vision, Tradition, Interpretation: Theology, Religion, and the Study of Religion* (Mouton de Gruyter, Berlin, 1988).

———, 'Faith and Culture in Interaction: The Alternative CSI Liturgy" in *Reflections (Festchrift for Rt Revd Sundar Clarke)* (Poompuhar Pathippagam, Madras, 1989).

———, *Healing Wings: Acts of Jesus for Human Wholeness*, artwork Jyoti Sahi, poems Jane Sahi (ATC, Bangalore, 1998).

———, 'Interpretive Dialogue with a Vaishnava Tradition' in *Spiritual Traditions: Essential Visions: Essays in Honour of David C. Scott*, ed. D.E. Singh (UTC, Bangalore, 1998).

———, 'Changing Eco-Faith Perspectives in India' in *The Bible Speaks Today: Essays in Honour of Gnana Robinson*, ed. D. Muthunayagam (ISPCK, Delhi, 2000).

———, 'All Loves Excelling: A Methodist Reflects on Hindu Faith' in *A Great Commission: Christian Hope and Religious Diversity (In Honour of Kenneth Cracknell)*, eds. M. Forward, S. Plant, S. White, (Peter Lang, Berlin, 2000).

———, 'Grace in Karnataka's Madhva: A Meeting Point for Christian Theologians' in *God of All Grace: Essays in Honour of O.V. Jathanna*, ed. J. George (ATC, Bangalore, 2005).

———, 'The Ecological Body: An Epiphanic Image' in *Mission with the Marginalised*, ed. S. Meshack (CSS, Thiruvalla, 2007).

McFague, S., 'Imaging a Theology of Nature: The World as God's Body' in *Liberating Life*, Birch, C. et al (ed.) (Orbis, New York, 1990).

———, *The Body of God: An Ecological Theology* (SCM, London, 1993).

Moltmann-Wendel, E., *I am My Body: A Theology of Embodiment* (Continuum, 1995).

Nehring, A., *Ecology: A Theological Response* (Gurukul, Madras, 1994).

Nirmal, A.P., 'Ecology, Ecumenics and Economy in Relation: A New Theological Paradigm' in *Ecology and Development: Theological Perspectives*, ed. D.D. Chetti (United Evangelical Lutheran Churches in India, Madras, 1991).

Overzee, A.H., *The Body Divine: The Symbol of the Body in the Works of Teilhard de Chardin and Rāmānuja* (CUP, Cambridge, 1992).

Polanyi, M., *Science, Faith and Society* (OUP, Oxford, 1946).

———, *Personal Knowledge* (Routledge, London, 1958).

———, *Knowing and Being* (Routledge, London, 1969).

Pope, G.U., *The Tiruvācagam of the Tamil Poet, Saint and Sage Māṇika Vācagar* (Clarendon Press, Oxford, 1900).

Radhakrishnan, S., *Indian Philosophy, 2nd Edition* (Allen and Unwin, London, 1931).

——— (ed. & trans.), *The Principal Upaniṣads* (Allen and Unwin, London, 1953).

Raghavachar, S.S. (ed. & trans.), *Vedārtha-Saṃgraha* (Ramakrishna Ashrama, Mysore, 1978).

Ramanujachari, R. (ed. & trans.), *Siddhi-traya of Yāmuna* (Madras, 1972).

Rao, T.A. Gopinatha, *Elements of Hindu Iconography, Vol. I, Part I* (Law Printing House, Madras, 1914).

Robinson, J., *The Body: A Study in Pauline Theology* (SCM, London, 1957).

Ruether, R.R., *Gaia and God: An Eco-Feminist Theology of Earth Healing* (Harper, San Francisco, 1992).

Sahi, J., *The Child and the Serpent* (Routledge, London, 1984).

———, *Stepping Stones: Reflections on the Theology of Indian Christian Culture* (ATC, Bangalore, 1986).

Sampatkumaran, M.R. (trans.), *The Gīta-Bhāṣya of Rāmānuja* (M. Rangacharya Memorial Trust, Madras, 1969).

Sastry, A.M. (trans.), *Bhagavad Gītā Bhāṣya of Śaṅkara, 7th edition* (Samata Books, Madras, 1977).

Selvanayagam, I., *Kristu Bhakti and Krishna Bhakti: A Christian-Hindu Dialogue Contributing to Comparative Theology,* (Christian World Imprints, Delhi, 2017).

Shiva, V., *Staying Alive: Women, Ecology and Survival in India* (Zed Books, London, 1989).

Sircar, M., *Comparative Studies in Vedantism* (OUP, Bombay, 1927).

Smart, N., *Doctrine and Argument in Indian Philosophy* (Allen and Unwin, London, 1964).

Srinivasacharya, K. (ed. & trans.), *Siddhi-traya of Yāmuna* (Madras, 1972).

Thibaut, G. (trans.), '*Śrī-Bhāṣya of Rāmānuja*' in *Sacred Books of the East. Vol. XLVIII*, ed. F. Max Muller (Clarendon Press, Oxford, 1904).

Varadachari, K.C., *Āḻvārs of South India* (Bharatiya Vidya Bhavan, Bombay, 1966).

Williams R., *The Edge of Words: God and the Habits of Language* (Bloomsbury Continuum, London, 2014).

Yamunacharya, M., 'Śaraṇāgati-gadya of Rāmānuja' in *Viśiṣṭādvaita: Philosophy and Religion, A Symposium by Twenty Four Erudite Scholars*, ed. V.S. Raghavan (Rāmānuja Research Society, Madras, 1974).

Young, F.M., *Construing the Cross: Type, Sign, Symbol, Word, Action* (Cascade Books, Eugene, 2015).

Zaehner, R.C., *At Sundry Times* (Faber and Faber, London, 1958).

———, *The Bhagavad-Gītā* (OUP, London, 1969).

INDEX OF NAMES

W

Y

Z